Primer on Anglo-American Law and Society

Lecture Notes

Ryan S. Song (송세련)

Table of Contents

I. Introduction [3]
    1. Goals and Objectives [3]
    2. Overview and Structure of the Book [4]

II. Law, Society, and Economy
    1. The Triadic Relationship of Law, Society, and Economy [7]
    2. Morality and Law [9]
    3. Utilitarianism and Categorical Imperative Reasoning [17]
    4. Society and Law – Florida Driver's License case [21]
    5. Law and Economy [23]
    6. American Legal Realism - Oliver Wendell Holmes, Jr. [25]

III. Historical Foundations of European intellectual tradition [27]
    1. Overview of European intellectual tradition (stick figure) [27]
    2. Dismantling of Great Chain of Being and Modernity [31]

IV. Civil Law and Common Law Tradition - Comparative look [39]
    1. Greco-Roman Origins of Civil Law [39]
    2. Development of Roman Law leading to Justinian Civil Code [40]
    3. Medieval Evolution and the Jus Commune [41]
    4. Enlightenment and Natural Law Influence [41]
    5. The Great Civil Codes: Napoleon and the German Civil Code [42]
    6. Characteristics of Civil Law System [42]

V. Early Development of Common Law [45]
    1. Overview of English Legal History [45]
    2. Before the Norman Conquest [46]
    3. Norman Conquest of 1066: Beginning of Common Law [48]
    4. Structural Development of Common Law [50]

VI. The Evolution of Constitutional Order	[55]
1. Introduction	[55]
2. Louis XIV and Absolutism: From Religious Wars to Revolution	[56]
3. The Tudor Dynasty and England's Path to Constitutional Monarchy	[57]
4. Comparative Analysis of Revolutionary Outcome	[63]
5. Republican Constitutionalism and State Reconstruction	[65]
6. Contemporary Constitutional Synthesis	[65]
VII. Development of Political, Philosophy and Capitalism	[67]
1. Political theories	[67]
2. Social Contracts	[67]
3. Development of Capitalism	[72]
VIII. American Legal Tradition – the Early Years	[75]
1. American law and society - A Complex Tapestry of Legal Culture	[75]
2. Overview of American Legal History in the Early Years	[77]
3. Constitution and Bill of Rights	[78]
4. Marbury v. Madison (1803) – Establishment of Judicial Review	[79]
5. Marshall Court and Federalism	[81]
IX. American Judicial system	[85]
1. Sources and Types of American Law	[85]
2. The Federal Court System	[86]
3. The State Court System	[88]
4. Stare Decisis: Stability and Evolution in Common Law	[90]
5. Common Law Legal Reasoning	[91]
X. Dispute Resolution – Trial	[95]
1. Case Studies	[95]
2. Judicial Procedure Before Trial	[98]
3. Trial	[101]
4. Appeals Process	[107]

XI. Supreme Court of the United States – a Primer	[109]
1. Overview	[109]
2. Jurisdiction of SCOTUS	[109]
3. Composition of the Court	[110]
4. Highly Political Nature of the Confirmation Hearing	[112]
5. Decision making process at the Supreme Court	[113]
6. Principles of Judicial Restraint in American Courts	[114]
XII. SCOTUS and Social Change: Warren Court	[117]
1. Warren Court and Civil Rights Movement	[117]
2. Earl Warren and his Appointment to SCOTUS	[119]
3. Milestone Cases of Warren Court - Expanding Civil Rights and Civil Liberties	[120]
XIII. Travails of Racial Equality	[127]
1. Origins of Legal Inequality	[127]
2. Supreme Court Decisions	[127]
XIV. 14th Amendment Protection of Civil Rights	[133]
1. Due process of Law	[133]
2. Equal Protection	[134]
3. Incorporation Doctrine	[135]
4. Modern Applications and Debates	[136]

Primer on Anglo-American Law and Society

Lecture Notes

Ryan S. Song (송세련)

CHAPTER I. INTRODUCTION

1. Goals and Objectives

This book's foundation rests upon several well-established premises regarding the interconnected nature of law, society, and economy. These systems do not exist in isolation but rather form an intricate web of mutual influence and dependency. The legal system is deeply embedded within its cultural context and historical development, which in turn reflects and shapes the broader intellectual traditions of Western civilization. Consequently, to understand a legal system is to explore the cultural heritage, historical evolution, and intellectual foundations of the society it serves.

My primary objective is to provide students with a comprehensive understanding of the Anglo-American legal system and its profound influence on American society. This understanding encompasses not only the technical aspects of law but also its broader social and cultural implications. The approach is deliberately multifaceted, examining the legal system through historical, cultural, and practical lenses. This system of law and thought affects virtually every aspect of society, from politics and economics to cultural values and social discourse, including both protected and prohibited forms of expression.

The book's methodology emphasizes practical problem-solving skills through the study of legal reasoning, while maintaining a broad perspective that situates legal developments within their historical and cultural contexts. To achieve these educational objectives, we explore several key areas of focus. First, we examine the internal relationship between law and philosophy, particularly concerning questions of morality and ethics. Second, we trace the historical development of Anglo-American common law and the judicial system, acknowledging the roles played by historical circumstances, influential leaders, and serendipitous events in shaping current legal institutions.

Furthermore, we provide an in-depth examination of trial processes, offering readers practical understanding for legal proceedings. Special attention is given to the United States Supreme Court, whose dramatic history and influential decisions have profoundly shaped American society.

Throughout this book, we strive to present this material in an engaging and informative manner, recognizing that the legal system is not an abstract concept but a living institution that affects our daily lives. Our goal is to equip readers with the knowledge and understanding necessary to navigate and appreciate the legal framework that shapes their everyday experiences. This practical approach ensures that readers will gain not just theoretical knowledge but also valuable insights into the legal system they encounter in their personal and professional lives.

By combining rigorous analysis with accessible presentation, this book aims to provide readers with a thorough understanding of how the Anglo-American legal system operates within and influences our society, while maintaining an engaging and informative approach that makes complex legal concepts accessible to all readers.

2. Overview and Structure of the Book

The Anglo-American legal system has profoundly shaped American society and life, weaving itself into the very fabric of the nation's cultural, political, and social framework. This influence is readily apparent in multiple spheres: the legal profession has provided a disproportionate number of the nation's political leaders, with a vast majority of American presidents, senators, and congressmen having formal legal training. The cultural impact of the legal system manifests in the significant number of movies, dramas, and books that center around courtroom proceedings and legal drama, reflecting America's distinctively litigious nature and the central role that legal processes play in resolving social conflicts.

This book traces the evolution of the American legal system from its historical roots in medieval English boroughs and towns through its transplantation to American soil with the arrival of the Mayflower. We examine the crucial early political battles between Federalists and their opponents that shaped today's centralized federal government and legal system. This historical foundation provides essential context for understanding contemporary American jurisprudence.

Following this historical survey, we explore the fundamental principles that distinguish American jurisprudence from other legal systems. These include cornerstone concepts such as due process, equal protection, and anti-trust laws, which form the bedrock of American legal thought and practice. The book then delves into the intricacies of trial procedures, providing a comprehensive examination of how lawsuits progress from initial filing through final resolution. This includes detailed analysis of pre-trial procedures, trial processes – including opening statements, examinations, and closing arguments – and post-trial proceedings such as appeals.

Special attention is devoted to the Supreme Court of the United States, arguably the most fascinating institution in the American legal system. We examine how the Court has positioned itself at the center of American life, exploring its evolution through significant eras including the Marshall Court, the Warren Court, and the contemporary Supreme Court. This section includes analysis of landmark cases that have shaped American society, particularly in areas such as racial equality and the right to counsel.

Through this comprehensive exploration, readers will gain a good understanding of how the Anglo-American legal system has evolved, operates, and continues to shape American society.

CHAPTER II. LAW, SOCIETY AND ECONOMY

1. The Triadic Relationship of Law, Society, and Economy

The legal system, society, and economy form an intricate web of interdependencies that shape human civilization. This chapter examines their dynamic interplay and mutual influence, demonstrating how changes in one domain inevitably ripple through the others. Flg.1 stylistically shows this relationship.

1) Historical Evolution

The relationship between law, society, and economy has evolved throughout history. Ancient civilizations developed legal codes primarily to regulate commerce and property rights, demonstrating the earliest links between economic activities and legal frameworks. The Code of Hammurabi, for instance, contained detailed provisions for commercial transactions, reflecting the sophisticated economic system of ancient Mesopotamia.

2) Legal Systems as Economic Facilitators

Legal systems serve as the foundational infrastructure for economic activity. Property rights, contract enforcement, and commercial law create the predictability necessary for markets to function efficiently. The development of corporate law enabled the rise of modern capitalism by facilitating capital accumulation and limiting liability. Similarly, bankruptcy laws balance creditor protection with economic renewal, illustrating how legal frameworks adapt to economic needs while maintaining social stability.

3) Social Influences on Legal and Economic Development

Social values and cultural norms significantly influence both legal development and economic behavior. Environmental regulations, for example, emerged from growing social awareness of ecological issues, subsequently reshaping industrial practices and creating new economic opportunities. Labor laws similarly reflect societal values regarding worker protection, directly impacting economic organization and business practices.

4) Economic Forces Shaping Legal Evolution

Economic developments often necessitate legal adaptation. The digital revolution has prompted comprehensive legal reforms in intellectual property rights, data protection, and electronic commerce. Similarly, globalization has led to the harmonization of commercial laws across jurisdictions, demonstrating how economic integration drives legal convergence.

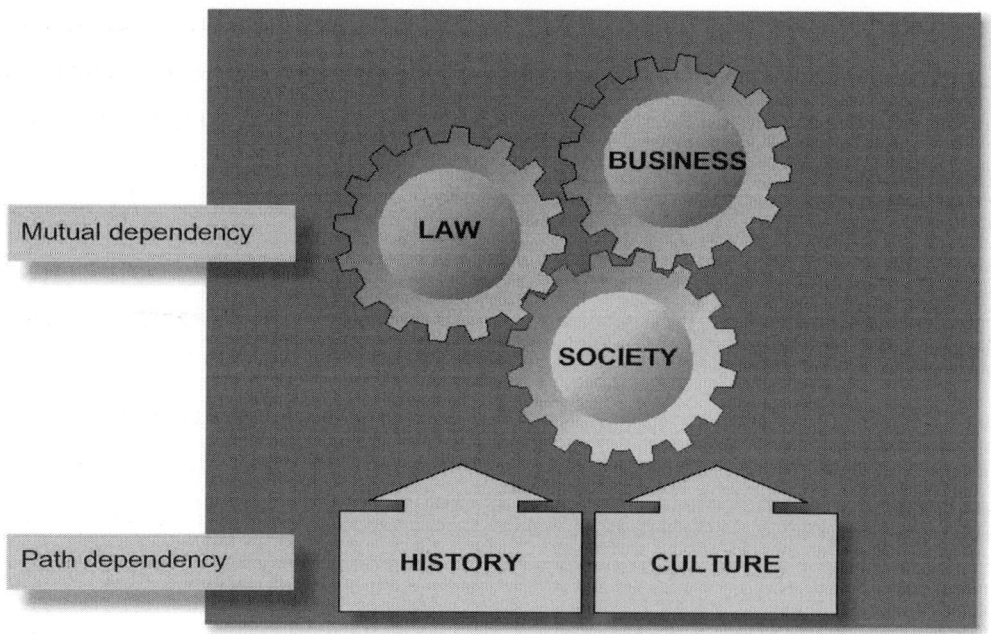

Fig. 1. Internal relationships among Law, Society and Economy

5) Social Consequences of Legal-Economic Interactions

The interaction between legal and economic systems profoundly impacts social structures. Taxation laws, for instance, influence wealth distribution and social mobility. Antitrust regulations shape market competition and consumer welfare. These legal-economic mechanisms significantly affect social equity and opportunity distribution within society.

6) Contemporary Challenges

Modern societies face complex challenges requiring coordinated legal, social, and economic responses. Climate change mitigation demands legal frameworks that incentivize sustainable economic practices while considering social impact. Similarly, technological disruption requires legal systems to balance innovation with social protection, highlighting the ongoing need for adaptive governance.

7) The Role of Institutions

Institutions serve as crucial intermediaries in this triadic relationship. Central banks, regulatory agencies, and courts must balance economic efficiency with social justice while operating within legal constraints. Their effectiveness depends on maintaining legitimacy across all three domains.

Understanding the interconnected nature of legal, social, and economic systems is crucial for effective governance and policy-making. As societies face increasingly complex challenges, solutions must account for the dynamic interplay among these three fundamental domains of human organization.

The implicit connections between the three spheres of our life and society are hinted at throughout the book, and readers are encouraged to pose questions repeatedly: How do advancements or modifications in one area impact and cause changes in other areas?

2. Morality and Law

1) How to think about law and morality

The relationship between morality and law stands as one of the most fundamental questions in legal philosophy, particularly within the Anglo-American legal tradition. This complex interplay raises crucial questions about individual conduct, societal welfare, and the proper role of legal institutions in mediating between competing moral visions.

The quest to understand morality in legal contexts necessarily begins with examining two primary philosophical approaches that have profoundly influenced Anglo-American legal thought. On one side stands Immanuel Kant's categorical moral imperative, which attempts to establish universal principles of moral behavior through reason alone, effectively secularizing traditional religious moral precepts without invoking divine authority. Kant's approach emphasizes the universality of moral principles and the inherent dignity of individual human beings. On the other hand, Jeremy Bentham's utilitarianism offers a more pragmatic perspective, focusing on consequences and seeking to maximize collective welfare through the principle of "the greatest good for the greatest number."

These competing philosophical frameworks continue to influence how we conceptualize the relationship between law and morality in modern liberal democracies. The tension between individual rights and collective welfare, between universal principles and practical consequences, manifests consistently in legal discourse and policy debates. The question of "what is the right thing to do?" must be answered both at the individual and societal levels, often yielding different and sometimes conflicting answers.

In liberal democratic societies, the law often functions as a mediating force between varying visions of substantive justice. This mediation reflects a fundamental characteristic of liberal systems: the acceptance that individuals may hold different moral views while still requiring a common framework for social cooperation. This recognition leads to an important distinction between legal and ethical arguments. While ethical discourse addresses what ought to be, legal reasoning primarily concerns itself with established agreements and precedents – how we have previously decided to address similar situations through law or contract.

The practice of law In Anglo-American systems thus operates within this tension between individual moral convictions and societal needs. Legal practitioners must navigate complex ethical considerations: what serves their client's interests, what maintains the integrity of the legal system, and what benefits society at large. These considerations often intersect with questions about the proper role of government – whether it should take a more paternalistic approach or maintain a lighter touch in regulating individual conduct.

These discussions inevitably lead to questions about the nature of freedom and liberty, concepts central to Anglo-American legal thought. Traditionally, these systems have placed significant emphasis on property rights as a foundation for individual liberty, but this raises further questions about the balance between economic freedom and social responsibility.

The separation between law and ethics in liberal societies does not imply their complete disconnection. Rather, it acknowledges that in pluralistic societies, law must sometimes function as a compromise between competing moral visions. This compromise reflects a practical necessity: the need for stable social ordering in the face of moral disagreement. Legal arguments, therefore, focus not on what the law should be but on how existing law applies to current situations.

This pragmatic approach to law and morality reflects a sophisticated understanding of social organization. It recognizes that while individuals may pursue their own moral visions, society requires a framework that can accommodate diverse ethical perspectives while maintaining order and protecting individual rights. The resulting legal system may not perfectly align with any single moral philosophy, but it provides a workable mechanism for resolving disputes and organizing social life in a pluralistic society.

The enduring challenge In Anglo-American legal thought remains balancing these competing demands: respecting individual moral autonomy while maintaining social cohesion, upholding universal principles while acknowledging practical constraints, and promoting collective welfare while protecting individual rights. This ongoing negotiation between morality and law continues to shape legal development and social progress in liberal democratic societies.

2) Cases and Thought experiments

As we examine the relationship between law and morality in more concrete terms, consider the following cases.

(1) Trolley Thought Experiment
(Hypothetical 1) You are an operator of a trolley car. Trolley with malfunctioning break hurls down the down-sloping track. At the end of the track, 5 workers. But the operator can turn the trolley car to a side track at the end of which is only one worker. Do you turn? What is the right thing to do?

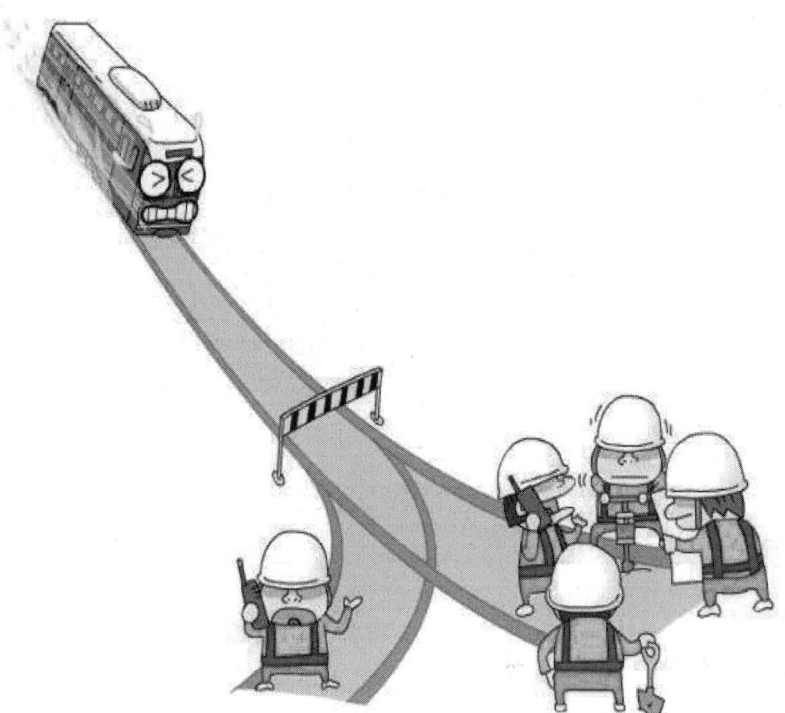

Fig. 1.

(Hypothetical 2) You are an on-looker on a bridge overhanging the track. Next to you is a fat man leaning over the bridge. You can shove him to cause him to fall directly on the track, killing him but stopping the trolley, and therefore saving the 5 workers at the end of the track. Do you shove the guy? Is the answer or principle different from the first hypothetical?

Fig. 2.

(Different hypothetical): You are a doctor. Five patients are injured lightly. One patient is severely injured. Severely injured person will take up time during which 5 people will all die. Do you attend to 5 people first, sacrificing the severely injured patient?
There's a healthy person who came in for a check-up. You can take out the organs of the person and save the others. Do you do it?

(2) The Queen v. Dudley and Stephens case (Regina v. Dudley[1]) – Fateful Boat Case

Fig. 3.

a) Facts as appeared in the decision:

"INDICTMENT for the murder of Richard Parker on the high seas within the jurisdiction of the Admiralty.

At the trial before Huddleston, B., at the Devon and Cornwall Winter Assizes, November 7, 1884, the jury, at the suggestion of the learned judge, found the facts of the case in a special verdict which stated "that on July 5, 1884, the prisoners, Thomas Dudley and Edward Stephens, with one Brooks, all able-bodied English seamen, and the deceased also an English boy, between seventeen and eighteen years of age, the crew of an English yacht, a registered

---

[1] Queen's Bench Division 14 Q.B.D. 273 (1884)

English vessel, were cast away in a storm on the high seas 1600 miles from the Cape of Good Hope, and were compelled to put into an open boat belonging to the said yacht. That in this boat they had no supply of water and no supply of food, except two 1lb. tins of turnips, and for three days they had nothing else to subsist upon. That on the fourth day they caught a small turtle, upon which they subsisted for a few days, and this was the only food they had up to the twentieth day when the act now in question was committed. That on the twelfth day the remains of the turtle were entirely consumed, and for the next eight days they had nothing to eat. That they had no fresh water, except such rain as they from time to time caught in their oilskin capes. That the boat was drifting on the ocean, and was probably more than 1000 miles away from land. That on the eighteenth day, when they had been seven days without food and five without water, the prisoners spoke to Brooks as to what should be done if no succour came, and suggested that someone should be sacrificed to save the rest, but Brooks dissented, and the boy, to whom they were understood to refer, was not consulted. That on the 24th of July, the day before the act now in question, the prisoner Dudley proposed to Stephens and Brooks that lots should be cast who should be put to death to save the rest, but Brooks refused to consent, and it was not put to the boy, and in point of fact there was no drawing of lots. That on that day the prisoners spoke of their having families, and suggested it would be better to kill the boy that their lives should be saved, and Dudley proposed that if there was no vessel in sight by the morrow morning the boy should be killed. That next day, the 25th of July, no vessel appearing, Dudley told Brooks that he had better go and have a sleep, and made signs to Stephens and Brooks that the boy had better be killed. The prisoner Stephens agreed to the act, but Brooks dissented from it. That the boy was then lying at the bottom of the boat quite helpless, and extremely weakened by famine and by drinking sea water, and unable to make any resistance, nor did he ever assent to his being killed.

Fig. 4.

The prisoner Dudley offered a prayer asking forgiveness for them all if either of them should be tempted to commit a rash act, and that their souls might be saved. That Dudley, with the assent of Stephens, went to the boy, and telling him that his time was come, put a knife into his throat and killed him then and there; that the three men fed upon the body and blood of the boy for four days; that on the fourth day after the act had been committed the boat was picked up by a passing vessel, and the prisoners were rescued, still alive, but in the lowest state of prostration. That they were carried to the port of Falmouth, and committed for trial at Exeter. That if the men had not fed upon the body of the boy they would probably not have survived to be so picked up and rescued, but would within the four days have died of famine. That the boy, being in a much weaker condition, was likely to have died before them. That at the time of the act in question there was no sail in sight, nor any reasonable prospect of relief. That under these circumstances there appeared to the prisoners every probability that unless they then fed or very soon fed upon the boy or one of themselves they would die of starvation. That there was no appreciable chance of saving life except by killing some one for the others to eat. That assuming any necessity to kill anybody, there was no greater necessity for killing the boy than any of the other three men." But whether upon the whole matter by the jurors found the killing of Richard Parker by Dudley and Stephens be felony and murder the jurors are ignorant, and pray the advice of the Court thereupon, and if upon the whole matter the Court shall be of opinion that the killing of Richard Parker be felony and murder, then the jurors say that Dudley and Stephens were each guilty of felony and murder as alleged in the indictment.

The learned judge then adjourned the assizes until the 25th of November at the Royal Courts of Justice. On the application of the Crown they were again adjourned to the 4th of December, and the case ordered to be argued before a Court consisting of five judges."

b) Questions to ponder..
- Is killing wrong under any circumstances?
- Is eating human being wrong under any circumstances?
- What is the right thing to do, apart from legal duties?
- Would consent exonerate them from moral violation?

3. Utilitarianism and Categorical Imperative Reasoning

1) Utilitarianism

Utilitarianism asserts that the moral value of any action is determined solely by its contribution to overall utility or well-being across society. This philosophical framework, most prominently championed by Jeremy Bentham, operates on the principle of maximizing "the greatest good for the greatest number," where good is typically conceptualized in terms of happiness or pleasure, and evil in terms of pain or suffering.

As a consequentialist ethical theory, utilitarianism evaluates the morality of actions based on their outcomes rather than the intentions behind them or the inherent nature of the acts themselves. The utilitarian approach fundamentally maintains that the ends can justify the means, provided those ends result in a net increase in aggregate human happiness or well-being.

This philosophical perspective represents a significant departure from traditional moral philosophies by proposing a relatively straightforward calculus for moral decision-making: one must simply determine which action will produce the greatest balance of pleasure over pain for all affected parties. This approach to ethics has profound implications for how we evaluate personal conduct, public policy, and social institutions, offering a systematic method for moral reasoning that continues to influence modern ethical debates and policy discussions.

2) Categorical moral imperatives (Deontological ethics)

Categorical moral imperatives, in stark contrast to consequentialist approaches like utilitarianism, evaluates the morality of actions based on their inherent nature rather than their outcomes. This ethical framework, most comprehensively developed by Immanuel Kant, is perhaps best encapsulated in the dramatic declaration "Let justice be done though the heavens fall!" - asserting that moral duties must be fulfilled regardless of their consequences. At the heart of Kant's deontological system lies the categorical imperative, which he articulated through three fundamental formulations.

The first formulation establishes universality as a criterion for moral action: one should act only according to principles that could reasonably become universal laws of behavior. This demands that moral agents consider whether their actions could coherently be willed as a universal practice for all rational beings.

The second formulation addresses human dignity, requiring that people be treated as ends in themselves rather than merely as means to achieve other goals. This principle establishes the fundamental moral worth of human beings and prohibits their instrumental use for others' purposes without regard for their own autonomy and dignity. The third formulation envisions moral agents as legislators in an ideal "kingdom of ends," where each person's actions contribute to a harmonious moral order respecting the autonomy and dignity of all rational beings.

These formulations together constitute a sophisticated ethical framework that continues to influence modern moral philosophy, offering a systematic approach to moral reasoning that emphasizes absolute moral duties over situational consequences.

Fig. 5. Jeremy Bentham and Immanuel Kant

3) Personalities

(1) Jeremy Bentham (1748 – 1832)

Jeremy Bentham was one of the most influential figures in English jurisprudence and moral philosophy during the late eighteenth and early nineteenth centuries. A child prodigy who began studying Latin at age three and entered Oxford at twelve, Bentham developed into a radical political thinker and legal reformer who fundamentally shaped Anglo-American philosophy of law. Although called to the bar in 1769, his frustration with the Byzantine complexity of English law—which he derisively termed the "Demon of Chikane"—led him to pursue reform rather than practice.

Bentham's intellectual legacy rests primarily on his advocacy of utilitarianism and his critique of natural law theory, famously dismissing natural rights as "nonsense upon stilts." His influence extended through his collaborators and students, notably James Mill and his son John Stuart Mill, and helped establish philosophical foundations for both modern welfare state policies and the concept of animal rights. His impact on education manifested in his role as the intellectual godfather of University College London. Bentham also gained recognition for conceptualizing the panopticon, an institutional building design that would influence future discussions of surveillance and social control.

Through his philosophical writings and social reform efforts, Bentham's utilitarian approach to ethics and law profoundly influenced subsequent generations of thinkers and reformers, including early socialist Robert Owen, establishing him as a pivotal figure in the development of modern legal and political thought.

(2) Immanuel Kant (1724-1840)

Immanuel Kant is a towering figure in Western philosophy, marking the culmination of Enlightenment epistemology that had developed through Locke, Berkeley, and Hume. From his home in Königsberg, Prussia—where he spent his entire life, never traveling more than a hundred miles from the city—Kant developed a revolutionary philosophical system that would influence thought well into the 21st century.

After enrolling at the University of Königsberg at age sixteen, Kant studied under Martin Knutzen, who introduced him to Newtonian physics and steered him away from both pre-established harmony theory and traditional idealism. This early influence helped shape Kant's later development of transcendental idealism, a distinctive philosophical position that differed significantly from the purely mental conception of reality found in traditional idealist thought.

Kant's masterwork, the Critique of Pure Reason, fundamentally reexamined the structure and limitations of human reason itself, while his subsequent works—the Critique of Practical Reason and Critique of Judgment—established groundbreaking frameworks for understanding ethics, aesthetics, and teleology. His profound reverence for both the "starry heavens above us, and moral law within us" epitomizes his unique ability to bridge the empirical and moral dimensions of human experience. Through these works, Kant established a new philosophical perspective that would reshape subsequent philosophical discourse on epistemology, metaphysics, ethics, and aesthetics.

4) Consider following criticisms to ponder regarding utilitarianism:
   - Utilitarian principle affected widely to the world where costs and benefit, market mechanism, capitalistic thinking reign supreme. But, whose utility should we consider?
   - Increase in society's utility does not guaranty even distribution of the benefit
   - In fact, unfair distribution of benefit can cause bigger social issues
   - How do you measure benefit and cost for different individuals? (extra money to a rich person can be a "nice to have", whereas the person who gave it up might be skipping dinner)
   - Would consent exonerate them from moral violation?
   - Is it just to sacrifice someone's utility to benefit the society?

5) Criticisms of categorical imperatives
   - But is the idea of Kant realistic?
   - Is killing wrong under any circumstances?
   - Is eating human being wrong under any circumstances?
   - What is the right thing to do, apart from legal duties?

6) Implications to legal profession
   - How should we incorporate morality into the law. How should we incorporate morality into our profession?
   - Suppose you are a defense attorney in a murder trial. Knowing where the body of the young girl is buried, her parents agonize over it and pleads you at least to let them know where the body is. Do you let them know?
   - In general, How would you defend the known criminal? Are attorneys just hired guns?

4. Society and Law – Mrs. Sultaana Freeman Case

1) Summary facts
   In February 2001, Sultaana Freeman, a Muslim convert, obtained a Florida

driver's license while wearing a niqab that revealed only her eyes, similar to her previous Illinois license. However, following the September 11 attacks, the Florida Department of Highway Safety and Motor Vehicles (DHSMV) demanded she take a new photo without the veil or face license revocation. When Freeman refused on religious grounds, her license was revoked, leading to legal action by the ACLU of Florida in January 2002.

2) Questions presented

The case raised fundamental questions about the balance between religious rights and state interests, specifically:
1. To what extent should religious beliefs be accommodated in government identification requirements?
2. What constitutes a compelling state interest in limiting religious expression?
3. How should courts balance security concerns with religious freedom protections?

3) Arguments

Freeman and the ACLU argued that the photo requirement violated Florida's Religious Freedom Restoration Act and the state constitution's free exercise clause, claiming it substantially burdened her religious practice without compelling justification. The state countered that public safety concerns, particularly the need for reliable photo identification for law enforcement, outweighed individual religious accommodations in this context.

4) Results

In June 2003, a Florida state court upheld the DHSMV's decision, finding that the photo requirement did not substantially burden Freeman's religious practice and that the state maintained a compelling interest in requiring unobstructed photo identification for driver's licenses. The ACLU subsequently appealed the decision in June 2004.

5) Implications

This case exemplifies the complex balancing act between religious freedom and public security concerns in post-9/11 America. It established that while religious beliefs deserve protection, they may be limited when they conflict with compelling state interests in public safety and law enforcement effectiveness.

5. Law and Economy: Dynamic Interaction

1) A Noxious Fox case (Pierce v. Post)

(1) Facts:
　　Post, a hunter, chased after a fox on a vacant beach and got it cornered and was just about to capture it, when Pierce, also a hunter, came out of nowhere, easily killed the fox and carried it away. Post sued Pierce for the value of the fox. The issue

presented was when and how one secures ownership over a wild animal.

(2) Procedural history:

The lower court awarded the value of the fox to Post, but on appeal, this case went all the way up to the highest court of the state of New York and was reversed. The issue was when does a person acquire a right of possession in a wild animal

(3) Reasoning:

Merely chasing it does not g/r/t occupancy and the right. Wounding, ensnaring, and circumventing the animal.. so as to deprive them of their natural liberty will establish the possession.

There was policy concern that the fox was a big problem at the time, because of it proliferation in the area. Justice Livingston reasoned that since the fox is a noxious problem, we want to encourage people to chase and kill those. But, if another comes along and simply takes the fruit of his labor (i.e., hunting), many will not go after the foxes. We need to award the efforts of the fox hunters.

Majority, however, preferred the bright line test for the case and decided on a method that is more expedient to enforce.

2) Notes on Economy and Law

The relationship between legal systems and economic modernization typically draws on Britain's historical development as the world's first industrialized nation. Max Weber's analysis of this phenomenon highlights an intriguing contradiction: Britain achieved unprecedented economic rationalization while operating under what Weber characterized as a "non-rational" legal system—the uncodified common law.

Weber's explanation for this apparent contradiction centers on the unique social positioning of English lawyers. He argued that their intimate connection with Britain's economic and social elite ensured the common law's dominance in the legal system. This close alignment between legal professionals and the ruling class,

Weber contended, resulted in a legal framework that actively supported business interests while restricting labor rights, thereby facilitating capitalist development. This occurred despite what Weber saw as the common law's conceptually irrational structure and its practitioners' pre-modern professional outlook.

6. American Legal Realism according to Oliver Wendell Holmes, Jr.

1) Expediency over Logic

Oliver Wendell Holmes, Jr. (1841-1935), a prominent American Jurist and legal scholar, who served Supreme Court justice from 1902-32 left the following insights on the role of common law in society:

"The life of the common law has not been logic; it has been experience. The felt necessities of the time, the prevalent moral and political theories, intuitions of public policy, avowed or unconscious, even the prejudices which judges share with their fellow-men, have had a good deal more to do than the syllogism in determining the rules by which men should be governed. ... The very considerations which judges most rarely mention, and always with an apology, are the secret root from which the law draws all the juices of life. I mean, of course, considerations of what is expedient for the community concerned."

For Holmes, the law's development is deeply embedded in social context, with judicial decisions being shaped by contemporary needs, prevailing moral and political philosophies, and the cultural perspectives shared by judges themselves. Perhaps most provocatively, he suggests that the most influential factors in judicial decision-making are often those least explicitly acknowledged – the practical considerations of community benefit that underlie formal legal reasoning.

This characterization stands in marked contrast to the Civil law tradition. Where Holmes describes common law as a product of accumulated experience, Civil law systems are built upon comprehensive, systematically organized codes that aim to provide logical, coherent frameworks for legal decision-making1. The distinction extends to fundamental approaches in legal reasoning: while Holmes emphasizes the role of practical experience and social context in common law development, Civil law traditionally employs deductive reasoning from general principles to specific cases2.

The role of judges also differs significantly between these systems. Common law judges, as Holmes describes them, actively shape the law through their experience and understanding of social needs. In contrast, Civil law judges traditionally play a more constrained interpretive role, focusing primarily on applying codified rules rather than developing law through experience and social considerations3. This difference is further reflected in the treatment of precedent – while common law builds upon accumulated judicial experience, civil law systems historically place less emphasis on previous decisions, though this distinction has somewhat diminished in modern practice4.

Holmes' perspective illuminates a fundamental tension in legal systems: the balance between logical systematization and practical experience. While civil law systems attempt to create comprehensive logical frameworks, common law, as Holmes describes it, explicitly acknowledges and embraces the role of social experience and practical considerations in legal development. This tension remains relevant today, as both systems continue to evolve and, in some ways, converge5.

2) Trends of railroad cases

Historians and legal scholars generally agree that, during the height of railroad construction (roughly the mid-19th century to the 1880s), courts often ruled in favor of railroad companies. The nation's political and economic priorities—encouraging rapid development and connecting distant markets—led judges to defer to the perceived "public good" these projects provided. However, once the major rail networks were established and public sentiment shifted—due to concerns over monopolistic practices, pricing abuses, and accident liabilities—lawsuits and regulatory actions began to favor individuals, smaller businesses, and state regulation.

CHAPTER III. HISTORICAL FOUNDATION OF EUROPEAN INTELLECTUAL TRADITION

1. Overview of European intellectual tradition (stick figure)

The intellectual heritage of Western civilization flows from two profound wellsprings: the philosophical traditions of Athens and the religious wisdom of Jerusalem. The first stream emerged from classical Greek and Roman thought, embodied in the works of towering figures like Plato, Aristotle, and Cicero. The second stream originated in Biblical teachings, flowing through the profound spiritual insights of Moses and Jesus.

These seemingly distinct intellectual currents converged powerfully in the works of the early Church Fathers, particularly Augustine, who began the monumental task of reconciling classical philosophy with Biblical revelation. This synthesis reached its apex during the medieval period, when thinkers developed sophisticated frameworks integrating faith and reason. This intellectual marriage produced both the systematic philosophical theology of scholars like Thomas Aquinas and the contemplative insights of mystics like Meister Eckhart.

The dawn of modernity, however, marked a decisive shift in how Western thought engaged with these ancient sources of wisdom. This new era would fundamentally redefine the relationship between classical philosophy and religious truth, establishing novel approaches to understanding both reason and revelation.

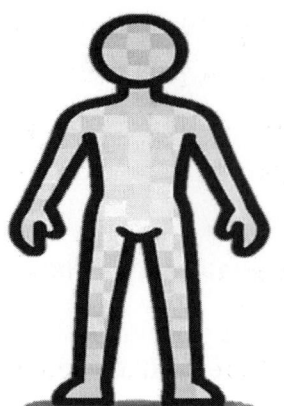

1) The anatomy of the West - The right leg represents biblical tradition.

The biblical foundation represents a persistent influence in Western thought and political development. Christianity has historically aligned with established social and political power structures. This tradition has significantly influenced major social movements, including the abolition of slavery, and continues to shape both conservative and reformist impulses in Western society.

2) The left leg represents classical tradition.

The Greco-Roman philosophical heritage has particularly resonated with secular intellectual discourse. This tradition emphasizes critical inquiry and rational examination, exemplified by the Socratic method. It raises fundamental questions about the relationship between philosophical thought and political governance.

3) The torso represents the "Middle Ages", the Christendom

The medieval period represents the integration of religious and classical traditions. This era attempted to reconcile faith with reason, demonstrated by instances where contemplative figures assumed administrative roles. The period produced systematic attempts to harmonize theological and philosophical perspectives.

The convergence of Athens and Jerusalem, catalyzed by Constantine the Great's acceptance of Christianity in the early 4th century AD, marked a pivotal moment in Western civilization. Constantine's conversion and subsequent policies, including the Edict of Milan in 313 AD, dramatically altered Christianity's status within the Roman Empire. This imperial patronage created an environment where Greek philosophical thought could more freely intermingle with biblical faith. While early Christian thinkers like Tertullian had questioned the compatibility of Athens and Jerusalem, Constantine's actions facilitated their fusion. The Church Fathers, particularly Augustine, emerged as Christian Platonists, adeptly using Greek philosophical concepts to articulate complex Christian doctrines such as the Trinity and the Incarnation. This synthesis was further solidified at the Council of Nicaea in 325 AD, which Constantine convened and presided over.

The council addressed theological disputes, resulting in the Nicene Creed, a statement of Christian belief that remains influential today. Constantine's involvement demonstrated the new intertwining of imperial power with Christian theology. The legacy of this convergence, initiated by Constantine's conversion, continues to shape Western thought. It represents not a victory of Athens over Jerusalem, but rather the beginning of an ongoing dialogue between reason and faith that characterizes Western civilization. This dynamic interaction between Greek philosophy and Christian theology would influence intellectual, cultural, and religious developments for centuries to come, forming the bedrock of Western intellectual tradition.

4) The left arm represents the Renaissance

The Renaissance period witnessed a renewed emphasis on classical humanism while maintaining Christian theological frameworks. This revival of classical learning occurred within, rather than in opposition to, Christian intellectual traditions.

5) The right arm represents the Reformation

The Reformation emphasized biblical authority while retaining classical philosophical concepts. This movement demonstrated how religious reform could occur while preserving elements of ancient philosophical thought.

6) The head represents modernity.

Modernity marks a pivotal shift in Western thought, characterized by a rejection of traditional authority, especially religious authority. This transformation redefined the concept of authority and reshaped the relationship between faith and reason.

Originally, authority was understood in a pedagogical context, with teachers as bearers of authoritative knowledge. However, modernity introduced a spirit of intellectual independence, challenging the notion that external sources could dictate one's beliefs.

This rejection of religious authority starkly contrasts modern and medieval worldviews,. The modern assertion that "no one can tell me what to believe" would have been considered foolish in medieval Europe, where clerics were tasked with instructing people in matters of faith.

Consequently, faith in modernity became increasingly privatized. Stripped of its medieval authoritative status, religious belief retreated into the realm of personal conviction. This privatization also led to a transformation in faith's nature.

In the modern context, faith often took on an emotional character, contrasting with medieval theology's more reason-based approach. This "matter of the heart" approach frequently manifested as a retreat from rational discourse into more subjective experiences, such as mysticism or fideism.

This reorientation of faith and authority in modernity significantly influenced Western social, political, and legal structures, contributing to the development of secular states and individual rights.

2. Dismantling of Great Chain of Being and Modernity

1) Great chain of being

The Great Chain of Being is a hierarchical structure of all matter and life, believed to have been ordained by God in medieval Christian thought. This concept organizes the universe from the highest form of perfection (God) down through angels, humans, animals, plants, and finally to minerals. Each level possesses the attributes of those below it, plus additional qualities. This Chirstian worldview influenced Western philosophy and theology for centuries, shaping views on nature, society, and morality. Dismantling of GCB marks the transition from the middle-ages to modernity.

2) The Crusades (1095 – 13thC, 9 campaigns)

When Seljuk Turks took control of Jerusalem (1070s AD) and reportedly harassing Christian Pilgrims to the Holy Land, Pope Urban II called for an armed pilgrimage to reclaim the Holy Land from Muslim control. The Crusades, while ostensibly religious military campaigns, served as a crucial catalyst for Europe's transformation toward modernity. These expeditions initiated unprecedented levels of East-West contact, exposing European society to advanced Arabic mathematics, classical Greek texts preserved by Islamic scholars, and sophisticated Middle Eastern trade practices. The Italian maritime cities, particularly Venice and Genoa, emerged as crucial intermediaries in this exchange, establishing trading posts throughout the Mediterranean and developing new financial instruments to facilitate international commerce.

This economic and intellectual exchange had far-reaching consequences. The influx of Eastern luxury goods created new markets and consumer desires in Europe, while exposure to Islamic scholarly traditions helped revive interest in classical learning. When Constantinople fell to the Ottomans in 1453, many Byzantine scholars fled to Italy, further accelerating the transmission of classical knowledge that would fuel the Renaissance. Thus, the Crusades initiated a chain of cultural and economic interactions that would ultimately contribute to undermining medieval European worldviews.

3) Black Death

Ironically, Italy was hit hard by the Plague due to its maritime trade, through bacteria carried by black rats. Also known as Bubonic plagues (1347-1351 initially but kept coming back to 17thC) claimed 1/3 to ½ of European population and caused people to think about death and human suffering. Artists depicted human conditions, emotions and reflections in their artworks. In the wake, people also thought about what constitutes "good life" in the midst of so much death. Many turn to classical, more humanistic texts and works.

The pandemic devastated religious orders as countless clergymen succumbed to the disease while fulfilling their pastoral duties of caring for the sick. This significant loss of religious personnel created immediate disruptions in church administration and spiritual leadership across Europe.

The demographic catastrophe triggered substantial economic changes. The dramatic population decline resulted in an acute labor shortage, causing wages to rise sharply as surviving workers gained unprecedented bargaining power. This shift in labor dynamics played a crucial role in undermining the feudal system, particularly the institution of serfdom, which had dominated medieval social and economic relationships. The scarcity of workers also led to an enhanced recognition of women's economic value, as their labor became increasingly essential in maintaining agricultural and commercial activities. These changes collectively contributed to the transformation of medieval Europe's social and economic landscape, helping to dismantle traditional feudal hierarchies and labor relationships.

4) The Renaissance: Architects of Modernity (14th to the 17th century)

The Renaissance emerged from a confluence of factors: the Crusades' exposure to Islamic scholarship, the preservation of classical texts in monasteries, and the devastating psychological impact of the Black Death, which prompted Europeans to seek new ways of understanding their world. The rise of wealthy Italian city-states provided the perfect incubator for this cultural transformation.

Key figures like Lorenzo de' Medici, whose patronage supported artists and scholars, helped establish Florence as the Renaissance's epicenter. Leonardo da Vinci embodied the period's ideal of the "Renaissance man," excelling in art, science, and engineering. Michelangelo's works, particularly the Sistine Chapel ceiling, revolutionized artistic expression. In literature, Dante Alighieri's use of vernacular Italian in "The Divine Comedy" helped legitimize local languages alongside Latin.

The Renaissance reshaped Europe by promoting individualism, scientific inquiry, and secular thinking. The invention of the printing press by Gutenberg accelerated the spread of knowledge. This intellectual revolution laid the groundwork for the Scientific Revolution, the Enlightenment, and ultimately, modern rational and empirical thought.

5) The Reformation (1517)

The Protestant Reformation, initiated by Martin Luther in 1517, emerged from growing dissatisfaction with Catholic Church practices, particularly the sale of indulgences for sin forgiveness. The immediate catalyst was Pope Leo X's fundraising campaign for St. Peter's Basilica through indulgences, which Luther vehemently opposed. His "95 Theses," originally intended for academic debate, spread rapidly throughout Europe thanks to Gutenberg's printing press, transforming a local theological dispute into a continental revolution.

Luther's core principles of "Sola Scriptura" (Scripture alone) and justification by faith fundamentally challenged the Church's authority and traditional religious hierarchy. His translation of the Bible into German democratized religious knowledge, previously controlled by the clergy. This radical shift in religious authority disrupted the medieval Great Chain of Being, which had structured society through divine hierarchical order.

The Reformation's impact extended far beyond religion. It fostered literacy through Bible reading, leading to the development of public education systems, including women's education. Luther's emphasis on individual faith and direct relationship with God inadvertently promoted egalitarian ideas that later influenced democratic movements. His concept of peaceful resistance to authority inspired later social reformers, from Martin Luther King Jr. to Mahatma Gandhi.

Politically, the Reformation fractured the Catholic Church's monopoly on power, leading to the emergence of nation-states and modern political institutions. It established precedents for civil disobedience and media's role in checking institutional power. The movement spawned numerous Protestant denominations, ultimately affecting over a billion people worldwide and laying groundwork for modern pluralistic society.

6) The Scientific Revolution: Transforming Worldviews (mid-16th to late-17th century)

The Scientific Revolution fundamentally transformed human understanding of the natural world and challenged centuries-old assumptions about the universe. This intellectual movement emerged from the Renaissance's revival of classical learning and the age of exploration's empirical observations, which increasingly conflicted with traditional Aristotelian and Ptolemaic models.

Nicolaus Copernicus (1473-1543) initiated this transformation by proposing a heliocentric model of the universe, explaining planetary motions more elegantly than Ptolemy's earth-centered system. Johannes Kepler (1571-1630) refined this model by demonstrating that planets move in elliptical rather than circular orbits. Galileo Galilei (1564-1642) provided empirical support through telescopic observations, revealing imperfections in celestial bodies that contradicted the ancient belief in heavenly perfection.

Isaac Newton (1642-1727) culminated this revolution by unifying terrestrial and celestial mechanics through his theory of universal gravitation. His work suggested an infinite universe, though this concept later conflicted with thermodynamic principles discovered in the 19th century.

This revolution's impact extended beyond science, challenging religious authority and traditional social hierarchies. It promoted rational inquiry and empirical observation as primary tools for understanding reality, laying foundations for the Enlightenment and modern scientific method. The resulting technological advances fueled the Industrial Revolution, fundamentally reshaping economic and social structures across Europe and eventually the world.

7) Renaissance Princes: The Transformation of European Monarchy and the Path to Modernity

The late medieval and early modern period witnessed a profound transformation in European monarchy, as rulers confronted multiple challenges to their traditional authority. While historically legitimized by the Great Chain of Being as God's lieutenants on Earth, monarchs faced increasing pressure from various intellectual and social movements that questioned this divine mandate.

The Renaissance introduced humanistic ideals and secular thinking, exemplified by Machiavelli's "The Prince," which approached governance through pragmatic rather than theological lens. The Protestant Reformation further eroded traditional religious authority, while the Scientific Revolution challenged fundamental assumptions about divine order. These movements collectively undermined the medieval worldview that had legitimized monarchical power through divine right.

In response, rulers adapted by developing new sources of legitimacy and power. They strengthened their position through strategic marriages, administrative reforms, and alliances with emerging urban merchant classes. This necessity for broader support led to the development of representative institutions such as the English Parliament, French Estates General, and Spanish Cortes. However, these bodies, initially created to facilitate taxation and maintain political stability, eventually became forums for negotiating power between monarchs and their subjects.

The period's economic challenges further complicated royal authority. The Ottoman conquest of Constantinople in 1453 disrupted traditional trade routes, forcing European powers to seek new economic opportunities and alliances. Monarchs responded by confiscating church properties, selling offices, and fostering colonial expansion, fundamentally altering the relationship between state power and economic activity.

This transformation marked the beginning of modern state formation, where legitimacy increasingly derived from effective governance and popular consent rather than divine authority alone. The emergence of an educated, politically aware populace, combined with new economic and social forces, laid the groundwork for later developments in constitutional monarchy and democratic institutions.

8) Maritime Exploration and the Spice Wars: Forging New Paths to Power

The age of maritime exploration (1415-1650) emerged from a confluence of political, economic, and technological pressures facing European monarchs. After the Ottoman Empire captured Constantinople in 1453, traditional eastern trade routes were disrupted, forcing European powers to seek alternative paths to the lucrative spice trade. This quest for new routes coincided with monarchs' growing need for independent wealth to consolidate power against noble factions.

Spices commanded extraordinary value in medieval and Renaissance Europe. Nutmeg from the Banda Islands (Indonesia) could be exchanged for seven oxen in 14th century Germany, while peppercorns could purchase a serf's freedom in France. Beyond culinary uses, spices were prized for medicinal properties and as luxury commodities, making them a crucial source of potential wealth for European rulers.

The ensuing competition for control of spice routes, known as the Spice Wars, transformed global commerce and politics. Portugal initially dominated these trade routes, followed by Spain, and later the Dutch and English. This competition spurred technological advancement in navigation and shipbuilding, contributing to the Scientific Revolution. The wealth generated from spice trade funded Europe's colonial expansion and religious wars, while also supporting the Renaissance and early modern state formation.

The challenges of modernity posed to the monarchs produced two contrasting responses, Constitutional Monarchy represented by England and the Absolute Monarchism seen in France. We will revisit this topic in Chapter VI (Constitutional Arrangements)

CHAPTER IV. CIVIL LAW AND COMMON LAW TRADITION – A COMPARATIVE LOOK

The Western legal world is primarily divided into two major legal families: civil law and common law systems. This fundamental division largely stems from their historical relationship to Roman law, with civil law systems developing directly from this ancient tradition while common law evolved independently in medieval England. These legal families represent distinctly different philosophical approaches and methodologies. Civil law systems typically employ a top-down approach, where abstract legal principles and systematic codes are deductively applied to specific cases. This reflects their origins in academic study and philosophical reasoning. In contrast, common law systems developed inductively from the bottom up, deriving general principles from specific cases and local customs over time.

This divergence is reflected in their traditional characterization: civil law as "written law" (jus scriptum), emphasizing comprehensive legal codes and systematic legislation, and common law as "unwritten law," building primarily on custom and judicial precedent. Understanding these fundamental differences provides crucial insight into how these legal systems approach justice, resolve disputes, and adapt to changing social needs.

1. Greco-Roman Origins of Civil Law

The foundations of civil law tradition can be traced to ancient Greek philosophical and rhetorical traditions, particularly their systematic approach to questions of justice and governance. Greek philosophers, notably Socrates, Plato and Aristotle, developed sophisticated theories about the nature of justice, law, and the relationship between individual rights and collective welfare. Their dialectical method of inquiry and logical reasoning became fundamental to later legal analysis and argumentation.

Greek city-states developed complex legal systems that distinguished between natural law (universal principles) and positive law (human-made rules). The Athenian legal system, with its public courts and citizen juries, established important precedents for procedural justice. Greek rhetoric, especially through schools like Isocrates', provided essential tools for legal argumentation that would later influence Roman advocates and modern civil law traditions.

This Greek intellectual heritage profoundly influenced Roman jurists, who systematized these philosophical principles into practical legal frameworks, ultimately forming the backbone of civil law tradition.

2. Development of Roman Law leading to Justinian Civil Code

The Roman legal system evolved from a simple set of customary rules to a sophisticated legal framework that would influence civilizations for millennia. This transformation began with the Twelve Tables (451-450 BCE), Rome's first formal codification of law, which established fundamental principles of private rights, judicial procedure, and equal justice under law. The subsequent development of praetorian law introduced crucial flexibility into the legal system, allowing adaptation to changing social and economic conditions.

A significant innovation was the distinction between jus civile (law for Roman citizens) and jus gentium (law applicable to foreigners), which helped Rome manage its expanding empire while developing universal legal principles. The classical period of Roman law saw the emergence of professional jurists who refined legal concepts and procedures through systematic analysis and writing.

This evolutionary process culminated in Justinian's monumental compilation, the Corpus Juris Civilis (529-534 CE). This comprehensive work, comprising the Codex (collected imperial legislation), Digest (juristic writings), Institutes (legal textbook), and Novellae (new laws), preserved centuries of Roman legal wisdom while adapting it to sixth-century Byzantine needs. The Corpus Juris Civilis would later serve as the foundation for civil law systems across Europe and beyond, establishing enduring principles of systematic legal codification and rational jurisprudence.

3. Medieval Evolution and the Jus Commune

Following the fall of Rome, much of classical legal knowledge might have been lost if not for Islamic scholars who preserved and commented on these texts during the European Dark Ages. This body of knowledge returned to Europe through Mediterranean trade routes and the Crusades, catalyzing a legal renaissance.

The formal revival began at the University of Bologna in the 11th century, where scholars like Irnerius initiated systematic study of Justinian's Corpus Juris Civilis. These scholars, known as glossators, developed sophisticated methods of textual analysis and interpretation, while their successors, the commentators, adapted Roman legal principles to medieval circumstances. This academic movement spread throughout Europe, establishing law as a university discipline and creating a class of professionally trained jurists.

The resulting legal framework, known as jus commune, emerged as a synthesis of Roman law, canon law, and local customs. Alongside this development, the rise of international trade fostered the lex mercatoria (merchant law), providing standardized rules for commerce. This period established the foundations of modern civil law methodology, particularly its emphasis on systematic organization, academic commentary, and the role of professional jurists in legal development.

4. Enlightenment and Natural Law Influence

The Enlightenment revolutionized legal thinking by emphasizing reason and natural law over traditional authority and divine right. Philosophers like Locke, Montesquieu, and Rousseau argued that law should reflect universal rational principles discoverable through reason. This intellectual movement challenged traditional legal authorities and pushed for systematic organization of law based on logical principles.

Natural law theory, asserting the existence of universal legal principles transcending human legislation, influenced codification efforts. The Prussian Allgemeines Landrecht of 1794 represented an early attempt to create a comprehensive, rational legal code reflecting these principles. This systematic approach to law laid the intellectual foundation for the civil codes that would follow.

5. The Great Civil Codes: Napoleon and the German Civil Code

The Napoleonic Code of 1804 and the German Civil Code (BGB) of 1900 represent two distinct approaches to modern legal codification. The Napoleonic Code, emerging from the French Revolution's ideals, emphasized clarity, accessibility, and practical application. It abolished feudal privileges, established equality before the law, and protected private property rights. Written in clear prose accessible to educated laypeople, it spread throughout Europe through Napoleon's conquests and voluntary adoption, influencing legal development across continents.

The BGB, in contrast, reflected a more scientific approach to legal organization. Drafted over two decades by legal scholars, it emphasized technical precision and theoretical sophistication. Its innovative "General Part" containing universal principles demonstrated its systematic nature. While more complex than the French code, its rigorous organization proved highly influential, particularly in East Asia where Japan adopted its approach, subsequently influencing Korean and Chinese law.

These codes exemplify different philosophies of legal organization: the French emphasis on practical accessibility versus the German focus on theoretical completeness. Their continuing influence shapes civil law systems worldwide.

6. Characteristics of Civil Law Systems

Civil law systems exhibit distinctive features that differentiate them from common law traditions, reflecting their historical evolution from Roman law and academic jurisprudence. A fundamental characteristic is their inquisitorial approach to judicial procedure, where judges actively investigate facts and question witnesses, contrasting with the adversarial system typical of common law jurisdictions where lawyers dominate proceedings.

The role of judges in civil law systems differs significantly from their common law counterparts. Civil law judges primarily interpret and apply codified law rather than creating law through precedent. They typically begin their careers immediately after law school and advance through a hierarchical judicial bureaucracy, unlike common law judges who are usually appointed after distinguished legal careers.

Legal doctrine and academic writing hold particular importance in civil law systems. Scholarly works often carry significant weight in legal interpretation, reflecting the tradition's academic origins in medieval universities. This emphasis on doctrinal analysis influences legal education, which focuses on theoretical understanding of abstract legal principles rather than case analysis.

Professional training similarly reflects these systemic differences. Civil law attorneys typically complete more extensive theoretical education but shorter practical training compared to common law jurisdictions. The profession often maintains closer ties to academia, with many practitioners contributing to scholarly publications and academic discourse, continuing the historical tradition of learned law.

CHAPTER V. EARLY DEVELOPMENT OF COMMON LAW

1. Overview of English Legal History

The overview below presents a concise timeline of English legal history, spanning from early Britain to the 12th century. It highlights key developments in the evolution of the English legal system, including the transition from local customs to centralized governance, the impact of invasions and conquests, and the emergence of common law principles.

Time line	Early Britain	~ 9c	~10c	~11, 12c	12c ~
	Local customs	Communal Justice	Personal Authority	Central government and King's Court	Beginning of common law system
Key driver	• Invasions	• Development of local community	• Rise of kings and strong feudal lords	• Norman Conquest (1066) and Strong central government	• Stationary royal court and recording of decisions
Description	• Ancient druids (priest-judges) drawing on Celtic customs • Romans, leaving Christian church and its customs (oath) – St. Augustine's mission from Rome (597 AD) • Otherwise, trial by ordeal prevailed • Danes left "Danelaw" from which the word "law" came from	• Administrative units (i.e., hundreds, villages, tithings) began to emerge • Administration did not distinguish legal procedure • Community kept their customs	• As England began more and more unification, strong kings and local lords dispensed their administration and justice • Still no coherent legal system • No records left	• King's justice was sought due to strong enforcement • King enjoyed the financial gains from fines and penalties • Itinerant administrators (juscariat) dispensed administration and justice (spreading common law) • King's court (Curia Regis) in Westminster	• Royal court and Benches began regular sessions at the same location (Exchequer) • Recordings began (Yearbooks in 13th C) • Lawyer as profession emerged • Local justice system organized

2. Before the Norman Conquest

1) The Absence of Roman Law Legacy in England

The Roman presence in Britain, spanning several centuries, left a significant mark on the island's culture and infrastructure. However, the legal legacy of Roman rule did not endure in England, primarily due to the abrupt withdrawal of Roman forces in the early 5th century. This sudden departure was prompted by the need to defend against the invasion of Attila the Hun on the European continent.

The vacuum left by the Romans' withdrawal paved the way for successive waves of Germanic migrations across Europe, including into the British Isles. These migrations, primarily by Angles, Saxons, and Jutes, transformed England into a predominantly Germanic realm. This transformation effectively erased much of the Roman legal influence, replacing it with Germanic customs and traditions.

2) Pre-Norman England: A Melting Pot of Influences

Before the Norman Conquest of 1066, England was a diverse region shaped by various cultural influences:

- Celtic and Druidic Traditions: The ancient Celts and their priestly class, the Druids, left their mark on early British customs.
- Roman Civilization: Despite the lack of legal continuity, Roman infrastructure and some cultural elements remained.
- Germanic Tribes: Angles, Saxons, and Jutes brought their own customs and legal traditions.
- Scandinavian Vikings: Norse influence was felt through raids and settlements.
- Christian Church: The arrival of St. Augustine's mission in 597 AD introduced Christian principles and canon law.

3) Early Legal Developments

The first surviving written laws in England date back to King Æthelberht I of Kent around 600 AD, coinciding with the Christianization of the Anglo-Saxon kingdoms. These laws, while primitive by modern standards, marked the beginning of a written legal tradition in England.

4) Anglo-Saxon Governance

Prior to the Norman Conquest, Anglo-Saxon kings had established a relatively efficient system of governance:

- The country was divided into shires, administered by shire-reeves (sheriffs).
- A system of written documents (writs) was used to standardize administrative matters.
- A permanent seat of government was established, with the royal treasury located at Winchester (later moved to Westminster).

5) The Norman Influence

The Normans, descendants of Viking settlers in northern France, had established connections with England long before the Conquest. King Æthelred's marriage to the daughter of the Duke of Normandy in 991 strengthened these ties. When William the Conqueror claimed the English throne in 1066, he brought with him Norman legal and administrative practices, which would significantly shape the development of English common law.

6) The Roots of Common Law

One crucial element that survived the various cultural shifts and became a cornerstone of the English legal system was the tradition of consulting "community sentiments" through gatherings of peers. This practice, born out of necessity in the absence of a centralized government, evolved into the jury system that became a defining feature of English common law.

In conclusion, while Roman law did not directly survive in England, the island's legal system evolved through a complex interplay of various cultural influences, culminating in the development of the unique English common law tradition after the Norman Conquest.

3. Norman Conquest of 1066: Beginning of Common Law

1) The Succession Crisis of 1066

The Norman Conquest of 1066 marked a pivotal moment in English legal history, precipitated by a succession crisis following the death of Edward the Confessor. Although Edward had designated Harold Godwinson—an influential nobleman, son of his advisor, and brother-in-law—as his successor, multiple claimants contested the throne. Among these challengers were Harald Hardrada of Norway, who based his claim on prior diplomatic arrangements between Edward the Confessor and Viking authorities, specifically an agreement between Harthacnut (son of Cnut the Great and Emma of Normandy) and Magnus the Great regarding mutual succession. William, Duke of Normandy, also known as William the Bastard, asserted his right to the throne as Edward's distant cousin, claiming that both Edward and Harold had previously pledged the crown to him.

2) The Twin Battles of 1066

The ensuing conflict unfolded in two dramatic phases. Initially, Harold Godwinson positioned his forces in southern England to counter the anticipated Norman invasion. However, when Harald Hardrada struck first, seizing York in the north, Harold was forced to respond with remarkable speed. His army covered 200 miles in just five days—an extraordinary feat of military mobility—to engage and defeat Hardrada at the Battle of Stamford Bridge. Yet this victory, though decisive, proved costly in terms of casualties and military resources.

The geographic and logistical challenges facing Harold's forces were immense. Immediately following their northern campaign, his exhausted troops had to march another 200 miles south within ten days to confront William of Normandy, who had landed in England shortly after the Stamford Bridge battle. This second engagement, the Battle of Hastings, resulted in Harold's death and Norman victory, fundamentally altering the course of English history.

The dual battles of 1066 had profound implications for English society and governance. Beyond the immediate decimation of England's noble class on the battlefield, the Norman victory reoriented England's political and cultural alignment away from Scandinavian influence toward Continental Europe, particularly France. This shift would later manifest in the extensive Anglo-French domains of Henry II, son of Matilda, who ruled over both England and substantial French territories.

3) Norman Influence on Legal Development

The Norman impact on English legal development was equally significant. Despite their adoption of French cultural elements, the Normans maintained their characteristic military discipline and centralized administrative approach. Their pragmatic methodology led to the systematization of existing legal traditions into what would become known as Common Law—literally, the law "common to all land." This legal framework emerged with distinctly practical characteristics: it developed through an inductive, bottom-up process, driven by the resolution of specific cases rather than abstract theoretical principles.

4) Characteristics of the Common Law System

This historical context helps explain several defining features of Common Law: its evolution through judicial dialogue and precedent (stare decisis), its practitioner-oriented nature, and its market-driven quality control mechanisms. Unlike Continental legal systems, which developed within more bureaucratic frameworks, Common Law emerged as a profession-based system where legal practitioners operated independently of civil service structures, subject to market forces rather than administrative oversight. While this approach sometimes resulted in less systematic development compared to Civil Law traditions, it proved remarkably adaptable to practical needs and local circumstances.

4. Stuructural Development of Common law.

1) William the Conqueror (1027-1087)

William I, the first Norman King of England, ascended to power through a combination of military prowess and strategic claims to legitimacy. His path to the English throne was shaped by his early experiences as Duke of Normandy, a position he inherited at age eight following his father's death in 1035. Despite the disadvantages of his illegitimate birth—he was born to Robert I of Normandy and his mistress Herleva, earning him the epithet "William the Bastard"—he successfully defended his dukedom against numerous challenges until firmly establishing his authority in 1060.

William's claim to the English throne rested on complex familial and political connections. The Anglo-Norman relationship had been strengthened in 1002 when King Ethelred of England married Emma, sister of Duke Richard II of Normandy, as part of a strategy to protect England from Viking raids. This marriage created a dynastic link that William, as Richard II's grandson, would later use to support his claim. Further legitimacy came from Edward the Confessor's apparent promise of succession in 1051, though this was contested by Harold Godwinson's claim that Edward had named him successor on his deathbed.

After securing victory at the Battle of Hastings in October 1066, William methodically consolidated his power, advancing northward to London while suppressing English resistance. His coronation on Christmas Day 1066 marked the beginning of Norman rule in England.

2) Henry II (1154-1189)

Henry II's reign represents a crucial period in the development of English legal institutions. As the son of Matilda (Henry I's daughter) and Geoffrey Plantagenet, he established the Angevin Empire, accumulating territories that made him more powerful than the French monarch. Through inheritance and marriage, he became Duke of Normandy (1150), Count of Anjou (1151), and Duke of Aquitaine (1152), before ascending to the English throne in 1154.

Under Henry's administration, the English legal system underwent significant systematization. He established permanent courts at Westminster—the Court of Common Pleas for civil matters and the King's Bench for criminal cases. His introduction of traveling judges (Eyres) promoted uniform law administration throughout the realm. The compilation of Glanville (1188), a comprehensive summary of laws and customs, marked a decisive shift toward common law supremacy over local jurisdictions. Perhaps most significantly, Henry initiated the jury trial system, gradually replacing traditional ordeals.

However, Henry's reign was marred by the infamous murder of Thomas Becket and internal family strife, leading to his eventual defeat by his son Richard I, supported by Philip II of France.

3) Edward I "Longshanks" (1272-1307)

Edward I, known as "Longshanks" due to his impressive height of 188 centimeters, significantly advanced both royal power and legal codification. His reign marked a period of intensive legislative activity, producing several foundational statutes that shaped English law.

He strengthened royal authority through the establishment of Parliament as a tax-raising body and the implementation of the Hundred Rolls inquiry into administrative abuses. The Quo Warranto proceedings, derived from these investigations, attempted to bring feudal liberties under crown control. Edward's legislative achievements were remarkable. The Statutes of Westminster (1275, 1285) codified existing law, while the Statute of Gloucester (1278) enhanced royal oversight of baronial rights. The principle that all liberties emanated from the Crown was formally established through the Statute of Quo Warranto (1290). This period of intense legal development, which included numerous other significant statutes, largely concluded with the death of his chancellor Robert Burnell in 1292.

Despite these legal achievements, Edward's military campaigns, particularly in Scotland, created significant financial and political tensions. His aggressive expansion nearly precipitated civil war as nobles resisted military service and taxation. The crisis was ultimately resolved through the Confirmatio Cartarum, which reaffirmed Magna Carta's principles while securing noble support for his Scottish campaigns.

5. Structural Development of Common Law

1) Juscariat

The Juscariat emerged in medieval England as a specialized legal society responsible for developing the common law. Centered in London, it comprised the Inns of Court where aspiring lawyers received training through lectures and apprenticeships. This system produced a cadre of legal professionals distinct from ecclesiastical and civil law practitioners. The Juscariat played a crucial role in shaping English legal traditions, fostering a unique approach to jurisprudence that emphasized precedent and practical experience over theoretical study.

2) King's Court (Curia Regis) in Westminster

The Curia Regis, or King's Court, originated in the early Middle Ages as a single royal court for most of England, situated at Westminster near London. Initially handling both administrative and judicial functions, it gradually evolved into a more specialized legal institution. The Curia Regis was the precursor to the later common law courts, including the Court of Common Pleas and the Court of King's Bench. Its development marked the centralization of royal justice and laid the foundation for England's unified legal system.

3) Exchequer and Recording of Decisions

The Exchequer, initially a financial department of the medieval English state, developed a significant judicial role. By the 13th century, it was established as a court of law, dealing primarily with revenue-related cases. The Exchequer was notable for its meticulous record-keeping practices, which included the systematic recording of judicial decisions. This practice of documenting cases and judgments contributed to the development of case law and the principle of precedent in English common law.

4) Lawyer as a Profession

The legal profession in England began to take shape around 1200, with a clear distinction emerging between advocates and attorneys. The profession grew rapidly, with the number of lawyers rivaling that of clergymen by 1700. The development of the Inns of Court in the 14th century provided a structured system for legal education and professional development. By the 18th century, lawyers had become influential social power-brokers, distributed throughout England and Wales, playing crucial roles in both urban and rural settings.

""

CHAPTER VI. The Evolution of Constitutional Order: A Comparative Analysis of English and French Monarchical Legal Systems

1. Introduction

The development of Western legal systems fundamentally diverged during the early modern period as responses to the crumbling of the Great Chain of Being, with England and France exemplifying two distinct paths toward modern state formation. This divergence, rooted in the respective reigns of Henry VIII and Louis XIII, established paradigms that would ultimately lead to dramatically different revolutionary outcomes: England's relatively peaceful transition to constitutional monarchy and France's violent rejection of absolutism. Through examination of their reigns and subsequent revolutionary periods—the Glorious Revolution (1688) and French Revolution (1789)—we can illuminate the foundational differences between Constitutional Monarchy and Absolute Monarchy, demonstrating how early modern legal frameworks influenced modern constitutional order.

Henry VIII's reign marked a crucial turning point in English constitutional development. His break with Rome through the Act of Supremacy (1534) established a precedent for Parliamentary involvement in fundamental constitutional changes. While Henry VIII wielded considerable power, his reliance on Parliament for major legal reforms inadvertently strengthened the institution's constitutional position. The dissolution of monasteries, though autocratic in nature, required parliamentary approval, establishing a pattern of cooperative governance between Crown and Parliament.

In contrast, Louis XIII's reign, particularly under Cardinal Richelieu's influence, concentrated power within the monarchy. The system of intendants, royal officials who directly represented crown authority in the provinces, bypassed traditional noble privileges and local parliaments. This administrative centralization laid the groundwork for the absolute monarchy that would reach its apex under Louis XIV.

2. Louis IXV and Absolutism: From Religious Wars to Revolution

1) The Genesis of French Absolutism

The aftermath of the French Wars of Religion (1562-1598) indeed precipitated a transformation in French governance, with absolutism emerging as a response to decades of civil strife. While the connection to Hobbesian philosophy is valid, it's worth noting that Leviathan was published in 1651, after the initial shift toward absolutism in France had begun. The monarchy had already started centralizing power under Henry IV (1589-1610) and Louis XIII (1610-1643), with Cardinal Richelieu playing a crucial role in strengthening royal authority.

2) Louis XIV and the Perfection of Absolutism

The famous attribution "L'État, c'est moi" to Louis XIV (1643-1715) is widely cited but historically disputed - there is no contemporary evidence he actually said these words. However, the phrase accurately reflects the essence of his governing philosophy. His conception of monarchy was indeed influenced by the Great Chain of Being, but more directly by the doctrine of divine right of kings, as articulated by Jacques-Bénigne Bossuet in his "Politics Drawn from Holy Scripture."

The Fronde rebellion (1648-1653) profoundly influenced Louis XIV's approach to governance. His experience as a young king during this civil war, particularly the humiliating flight from Paris in 1649, shaped his determination to prevent noble opposition through a combination of coercion and co-optation.

3) Versailles as a Political Instrument

The transformation of Versailles from a hunting lodge to a magnificent palace served multiple political purposes beyond mere display. It was a sophisticated instrument of political control, requiring nobles to reside at court where they could be monitored and managed. The palace's elaborate etiquette and ceremony weren't simply displays of grandeur but mechanisms for occupying the nobility with matters of precedence and ritual rather than political opposition.

4) Economic and Administrative Reality

While Louis XIV's reign witnessed periods of economic prosperity under Jean-Baptiste Colbert's administration (1665-1683), the financial strain came primarily from nearly continuous warfare rather than palace building or court expenditures. The Wars of Devolution (1667-1668), Dutch War (1672-1678), War of the League of Augsburg (1688-1697), and War of Spanish Succession (1701-1714) progressively exhausted French resources.

The relationship between Louis XIV's reign and the French Revolution needs more nuanced consideration. While the immediate causes of the Revolution emerged from the specific crisis of the 1780s under Louis XVI, including failed attempts at reform, agricultural crises, and the impact of American Revolution ideas, Lous XIV's centralization of power and fiscal policies did contribute to long-term structural problems.

5) Legacy and Historical Significance

Louis XIV's model of absolutism influenced European governance well into the 18th century, with rulers from Prussia to Russia emulating aspects of his system. However, its success depended heavily on the king's personal capabilities and engagement with governance - qualities that his successors Louis XV and Louis XVI notably lacked.

This revised analysis provides a more precise understanding of French absolutism's development, implementation, and consequences, while maintaining proper chronological perspective on its relationship to both the Wars of Religion and the French Revolution.

3. The Tudor Dynasty and England's Path to Constitutional Monarchy

1) Henry VII and the End of the Wars of the Roses

While continental Europe responded to the crisis of authority through absolutism, England evolved toward constitutional monarchy through a distinct historical trajectory. This process began with Henry VII (1457-1509), founder of the

Tudor dynasty, whose ascension marked the conclusion of the Wars of the Roses. Born into complex dynastic connections—his mother Margaret Beaufort descended from the Lancastrian branch of the Plantagenets, while his father Edmund Tudor was both half-brother to Henry VI and heir to Welsh noble lineage—Henry VII's claim to the throne emerged from both heritage and conquest.

The Wars of the Roses, a series of civil conflicts between the Houses of Lancaster and York, shaped Henry's path to power. Following his uncle Henry VI's defeat by Edward IV in 1471, Henry spent fourteen years in exile in Brittany. The political instability of the period reached its apex when Richard III seized power from his young nephew Edward V, allegedly ordering the murders of both Edward and his brother in the Tower of London. This act of usurpation catalyzed noble opposition, enabling Henry Tudor to gather support for his eventual victory over Richard III at the Battle of Bosworth Field in 1485. His subsequent marriage to Elizabeth of York strategically united the warring houses, though his reign remained characterized by persistent anxiety over potential noble conspiracies.

2) Henry VIII and the Transformation of English Monarchy

Henry VIII's reign (1509-1547) marked a pivotal transition in English governance and religious authority. Though initially maintaining Catholic orthodoxy, his growing desire for ecclesiastical autonomy would fundamentally reshape the relationship between church and state in England. This transformation was driven largely by dynastic concerns—the legacy of civil war made securing male succession paramount in Henry's political calculations.

Ascending to the throne at eighteen, Henry VIII initially embodied Renaissance ideals of kingship, combining physical prowess with intellectual accomplishment. His extraordinary wealth, manifested in a vast network of royal residences numbering between fifty and sixty palaces, demonstrated the Tudor monarchy's consolidation of power. However, a severe jousting accident in 1536 marked a crucial turning point. The resulting chronic leg ulcer not only affected his physical health but also appeared to influence his temperament and decision-making in later years.

3) The Emergence of Constitutional Principles

The evolution toward constitutional monarchy under the Tudors, while predating John Locke's formal political philosophy, established crucial precedents for later constitutional development. Henry VIII's break with Rome, though motivated by personal and dynastic concerns, required parliamentary cooperation, thereby inadvertently strengthening England's representative institutions. This process created a framework for the later development of constitutional monarchy, distinctly different from the absolutist model pursued by continental European monarchs.

This transformation exemplifies how England's unique historical circumstances—including the aftermath of civil war, dynastic insecurity, and religious reformation—contributed to a gradual limitation of royal power through institutional development rather than revolutionary change. The Tudor period thus laid the groundwork for England's distinctive path toward constitutional governance, though the full realization of these principles would require several more centuries of political evolution.

4) Six wives of Henry VIII

(1) 1st Wife: Catherine of Aragon (1485-1536) - divorced

Initially married to Henry's brother Arthur, Catherine wed Henry VIII in 1509 after Arthur's death. Their 24-year marriage was supported by biblical justification from Deuteronomy 25:5. Despite bearing Mary Tudor, she failed to produce a male heir, leading to Henry's pursuit of divorce. This catalyzed England's break with Rome and establishment of the Anglican Church. Catherine died in isolation at Kimbolton Castle, forbidden from seeing her daughter.

(2) 2nd Wife: Anne Boleyn (1501-1536) - beheaded

Anne Boleyn transformed from lady-in-waiting to queen, catalyzing England's religious reformation. Though she bore future Queen Elizabeth I, her failure to produce a male heir and miscarriage of a son in 1536 led to her downfall. Living in great luxury with a staff of 250, her reign ended dramatically when Thomas Cromwell orchestrated charges of treason, incest, and adultery. Henry arranged a French executioner for a swift beheading.

(3) 3rd Wife: Jane Seymour (1508-1537) - died shortly after a cesarean birth of Edward VI

Henry's favorite wife served as lady-in-waiting to Anne Boleyn before becoming queen. She successfully provided Henry's long-desired male heir, Edward VI, in 1537. As a devout Catholic, she worked diligently to reconcile Henry with his daughter Mary and advocated for Elizabeth's better treatment. Her triumph was short-lived, as she died shortly after Edward's birth, possibly due to complications from a cesarean section.

(4) 4th Wife: Anne of Cleves (1515-1557) - divorced

Anne's marriage was orchestrated by Thomas Cromwell to strengthen Protestant alliances during the English Reformation. After seeing Hans Holbein's flattering portrait, Henry agreed to the match but found her unappealing in person. Despite proceeding with the marriage for diplomatic reasons, Henry never consummated it. The six-month union ended amicably, with Anne accepting generous settlement terms and becoming the "King's Sister."

(5) 5th Wife: Catherine Howard (1521-1542) - beheaded

The young and beautiful Catherine Howard, Anne Boleyn's cousin, became Henry's fifth wife after serving as lady-in-waiting to Anne of Cleves. While Henry was enamored with his "rose without a thorn," Catherine found little attraction to the aging, obese king. Her affair with Thomas Culpeper led to her arrest, torture, and execution for treason, marking another tragic chapter in Henry's marital history.

(6) 6th Wife: Catherine Parr (1512-1548) - widowed

Catherine Parr, an intelligent and wealthy widow, brought stability to Henry's final years. Married at 31 to the 52-year-old king, she effectively managed royal affairs during his military campaigns and skillfully navigated court politics. Her competence in caring for the aging Henry earned his trust and admiration. After his death, she became one of England's wealthiest individuals before marrying Thomas Seymour.

5) Henry VIII and The Evolution of Parliamentary Power in England

(1) Origins and Early Development

Parliament originated as a pragmatic assembly of regional merchants and nobles who negotiated tax matters with the monarchy. This limited fiscal role expanded dramatically during Henry VIII's reign, particularly through the religious upheaval surrounding the establishment of the Anglican Church and his marriage to Anne Boleyn. These events necessitated parliamentary approval, inadvertently broadening Parliament's scope of authority.

(2) Institutional Development and Balance of Power

The transformation of Parliament from a tax-consultation body to a genuine political institution created an unprecedented system of checks and balances between monarch and representatives. Though these representatives primarily served noble interests, their growing influence led to the development of legal frameworks restricting royal power. This process elevated documents like the Magna Carta and later the Bill of Rights to constitutional status, despite their original contexts being quite different from their eventual significance.

A distinctive feature of English political development was the emergence of a negotiation-based relationship between Crown and Parliament. This culture of political compromise and discussion markedly differed from continental European practices, where absolute royal sovereignty remained dominant. The English approach notably resulted in relatively bloodless political transitions, exemplified by the Glorious Revolution of 1688.

(3) Legal Theory and Constitutional Development

The rejection of absolute royal sovereignty found theoretical support in common law jurisprudence. As Chief Justice Coke articulated in 1611, royal prerogative was limited to "that which the law of the land allows." This principle, though revolutionary for its time, built upon existing legal traditions, creatively interpreting documents like the Magna Carta to support emerging concepts of fundamental liberties and human rights. This legal framework significantly influenced later constitutional developments, including the United States Constitution's due process provisions, establishing a lasting legacy in Anglo-American legal thought.

6) The English Reformation: Politics, Religion, and Power

The English Reformation of 1534, while nominally sparked by Henry VIII's desire to annul his marriage to Catherine of Aragon, emerged within a broader context of religious reform sweeping across Europe. Though initially driven by Henry's personal motivations, the movement gained momentum through existing Protestant sympathizers who sought independence from Roman Catholic authority.

(1) Key Figures and Their Fates

Thomas More

As Lord Chancellor succeeding Wolsey, Thomas More stood firmly against both the annulment and the break with Rome, ultimately paying for his convictions with his life. His execution in 1535 on charges of high treason, orchestrated by Thomas Cromwell, marked a pivotal moment in the reformation's progression. More's legacy proved enduring—his philosophical work "Utopia" influenced later socialist thought, and he achieved the rare distinction of canonization by both the Roman Catholic (1935) and Anglican (1980) churches.

Thomas Cromwell

Thomas Cromwell emerged as the primary architect of the English Reformation, combining legal expertise with political acumen to engineer both the establishment of the Anglican Church and Henry's first marriage annulment. As chief minister (1532-1540), he wielded unprecedented influence but became entangled in court politics. His conflict with Anne Boleyn over monastery assets led him to orchestrate her downfall, while his ill-fated arrangement of Henry's marriage to Anne of Cleves ultimately precipitated his own execution in 1540.

(2) Historical Significance

The English Reformation represents a crucial intersection of personal, political, and religious motivations that fundamentally reshaped English society. The fates of More and Cromwell illustrate the period's volatility, where principled opposition and political miscalculation could prove equally fatal. Their contrasting approaches to the religious changes—More's principled resistance versus Cromwell's pragmatic implementation—exemplify the complex moral and political choices faced by Tudor England's leading figures.

4. Comparative Analysis of Revolutionary Outcomes

1) The Glorious Revolution: Constitutional Evolution

The Glorious Revolution of 1688 represented the culmination of England's gradual constitutional development. The Bill of Rights (1689) codified limitations on royal power that had roots in Henry VIII's era, particularly, parliamentary supremacy in legislation, regular parliamentary sessions, and restrictions on royal prerogative. These developments evolved from, rather than completely rejected, earlier legal traditions.

2) The French Revolution: Systemic Rupture

The French Revolution, occurring a century later, represented a complete break with the absolutist system. The absence of effective intermediate institutions between monarch and subjects—partially due to policies initiated under Louis XIII—left no framework for gradual reform. The Declaration of the Rights of Man and Citizen (1789) had to construct new legal principles rather than codify existing traditions.

3) Implications for Modern Constitutionalism

The divergent evolutionary paths of English and French constitutional development continue to shape modern legal systems and governance structures in profound ways. This influence extends beyond their respective nations to impact global constitutional thought and practice.

The English model demonstrates several enduring principles that influence modern constitutional systems. At its core, institutional adaptation represents a fundamental characteristic of this model, wherein historical institutions are preserved while their functions evolve to meet contemporary needs. This process facilitates the integration of traditional authority structures within modern democratic frameworks, while simultaneously allowing for the development of unwritten constitutional conventions alongside formal legal structures.

The distribution of power within this system emerged through organic institutional development, establishing effective checks and balances that continue to influence modern governance. Intermediate bodies play a crucial role in mediating between state and society, demonstrating the importance of gradual reform in maintaining systemic stability. This evolutionary approach has proven particularly effective in preserving legitimate authority while adapting to changing social and political circumstances.

The continuity of legal tradition remains a defining feature of this model, as common law principles have been successfully incorporated into modern constitutional frameworks. This integration has facilitated the development of judicial review while maintaining parliamentary supremacy, creating a sophisticated balance between written and unwritten constitutional elements that provides both flexibility and stability.

5. Republican Constitutionalism and State Reconstruction

The French experience has provided equally important lessons for modern constitutional systems. The relationship between state centralization and democratic accountability emerges as a central theme, manifesting in the role of bureaucratic structures in modern governance and the persistent tension between administrative efficiency and local autonomy. This centralized approach has significantly influenced how modern states conceptualize and implement administrative authority.

Rights-based constitutionalism, emerging from the French revolutionary tradition, has fundamentally shaped modern constitutional thinking. The emergence of universal rights declarations as constitutional foundations has established a framework for developing abstract principles into concrete legal rights, while simultaneously addressing the complex relationship between individual rights and state sovereignty. This rights-centered approach continues to influence constitutional development worldwide.

The dynamics of constitutional change revealed through the French experience highlight the challenges of establishing stable constitutional systems through revolutionary transformation. The role of written constitutions in establishing new political orders and the importance of building legitimate institutions after systemic rupture remain crucial considerations in modern constitutional design.

6. Contemporary Constitutional Synthesis

Modern constitutional systems often reflect a sophisticated synthesis of both traditions. Institutional design in contemporary systems demonstrates the delicate balance between traditional legitimacy and democratic accountability, while successfully integrating rights-based frameworks with practical governance structures. The tension between centralization and subsidiarity continues to shape institutional arrangements across different constitutional systems.

The evolution of legal frameworks in modern states reflects this synthesis through the development of mixed systems incorporating multiple legal traditions. Contemporary constitutional structures demonstrate remarkable adaptability in reconciling historical institutions with modern democratic requirements, while simultaneously evolving new constitutional forms to address emerging challenges.

The question of democratic legitimacy remains central to modern constitutional systems, as they strive to reconcile popular sovereignty with institutional stability. Modern constitutions have developed increasingly sophisticated mechanisms for constitutional change and adaptation, seeking an optimal balance between constitutional rigidity and flexibility. This ongoing process of constitutional evolution demonstrates the enduring influence of both the English and French models on contemporary governance structures.

This comparative analysis ultimately suggests that successful constitutional systems depend not merely on their formal structures but on their relationship to pre-existing legal traditions and institutions. The contrasting experiences of England and France continue to inform debates about constitutional design, institutional reform, and the relationship between historical legitimacy and democratic governance in contemporary legal systems worldwide.

CHAPTER VII. DEVELOPMENT OF POLITICAL PHILOSOPHY AND CAPITALISM

1. Political theories

The departure from the medieval concept of the Great Chain of Being marked a revolutionary transformation in political thought, particularly exemplified through the works of Niccolò Machiavelli (1469-1527). In his groundbreaking political treatises, Machiavelli departed radically from the traditional theological framework that had dominated European political philosophy for centuries. Rather than deriving political legitimacy from divine ordination, as prescribed by the Great Chain of Being doctrine, Machiavelli proposed a pragmatic and secular approach to political power. His writings, particularly "The Prince," emphasized that political authority stemmed from a ruler's ability to cultivate and maintain power through practical means, strategic thinking, and careful management of public perception.

This marked a significant intellectual break from medieval political theology, where legitimate rule was understood as flowing downward from God through a divinely ordained hierarchical structure. Machiavelli's revolutionary proposition suggested that political power was fundamentally self-made, acquired through calculated action rather than divine appointment. A ruler's effectiveness, in his view, depended not on moral virtue or divine blessing but on their capacity to inspire fear and command respect through strategic governance. The erosion of the Great Chain of Being concept subsequently gave rise to two major competing theories of political legitimacy: the social contract theories developed by Thomas Hobbes and John Locke.

2. Social Contracts

1) Thomas Hobbes (1588-1679)

Thomas Hobbes applied the emerging scientific method to questions of government and society. Writing in the aftermath of the English Civil War, Hobbes sought to understand political authority not through traditional religious or classical philosophical frameworks, but through systematic observation of human nature. His masterwork, Leviathan (1651), presents perhaps the first purely secular justification for absolute political authority. He is called a Philosopher of Fear

(1) Scientific Approach to Human Nature

Unlike his medieval predecessors who relied on Biblical interpretation or classical authorities, Hobbes approached political philosophy as a scientist would approach natural phenomena. Just as Galileo observed the motion of planets or Newton studied gravity, Hobbes attempted to derive political principles from careful observation of human behavior. Through these observations, Hobbes concluded that humans are fundamentally driven by passions, appetites, and physical needs rather than reason or moral sentiment. More controversially, he argued that humans will inevitably pursue these desires at the expense of others when unconstrained by political authority.

(2) The State of Nature and Social Contract

This understanding of human nature led to Hobbes' famous characterization of life in the "state of nature" - the hypothetical condition before political society - as "solitary, poor, nasty, brutish, and short." In this pre-political condition, humans exist in a "war of all against all" where no one's life or property is secure. The constant threat of violence makes agriculture, commerce, science, and civilization impossible. Importantly, this conflict arises not from human evil but from rational self-interest - in the absence of common authority, attacking first is often the safest strategy.

The solution, Hobbes argued, comes through a social contract where individuals collectively agree to surrender their natural rights to an absolute sovereign. This sovereign (whether an individual monarch or assembly) must have unlimited power to create and enforce laws, as any limitation would reintroduce the instability of the state of nature. While this sovereign might become tyrannical, Hobbes argued that even the worst tyranny would be preferable to the chaos of nature.

(3) Breaking with Tradition

Hobbes' theory marked a decisive break with traditional justifications for political authority. Rather than grounding legitimacy in divine right or natural law, Hobbes based it entirely on a rational social contract arising from human self-interest. Power originates from the people's calculated decision to create government, not from God or tradition. However, once established, this transfer of authority is irrevocable - subjects cannot withdraw their consent without dissolving society itself. This secular foundation for absolute authority found its most famous expression in Louis XIV's declaration "L'État, c'est moi" ("I am the State").

(4) Impact on Political Theory

Although Hobbes advocated for absolute monarchy, his methodology and core concepts profoundly influenced the development of constitutional theory. By establishing the social contract, and therefore rational consent, as the basis for political legitimacy, Hobbes provided tools that later theorists would use to argue for limited government and individual rights.

Several key Hobbesian innovations proved crucial for constitutional thought:

First, his insistence that political authority originates from the people, even if immediately transferred to a sovereign, established popular sovereignty as the foundation of legitimate government. This principle would become central to constitutional theory, though interpreted very differently by subsequent thinkers, such as John Locke.

Second, Hobbes' focus on the protective function of government - that its primary purpose is securing peace and safety for citizens - provided a standard against which governmental performance could be judged. While Hobbes believed only absolute power could achieve this goal, later theorists would argue that limited, constitutional government could better secure citizens' rights and interests.

Third, his systematic method of analyzing political questions through reason rather than tradition or revelation helped establish a framework for thinking about constitutional design. The idea that political institutions should be judged by their practical effects rather than their conformity to traditional models proved essential for constitutional innovation.

2) John Locke (1632-1704)

John Locke developed a theory of political authority that would become the intellectual foundation for constitutional democracy and limited government. His most influential political works, the Two Treatises of Government (1690), emerged from his experience during the political climate of Restoration England. While building on Hobbes's idea of the social contract, Locke reached radically different conclusions about the nature and limits of legitimate political authority.

(1) A More Optimistic View of Human Nature

Unlike Hobbes, who saw humans as naturally prone to conflict, Locke began with a fundamentally more optimistic view of human nature. In his Essay Concerning Human Understanding, he argued that humans are born neither good nor evil but as "blank slates" (tabula rasa) shaped by their experiences and environment. This rejection of innate depravity had profound implications for political theory. If humans are naturally capable of reason and moral behavior, Locke argued, they don't require absolute authority to prevent social collapse.

Locke believed that human reason, when properly developed, leads naturally to understanding of moral truth and even religious knowledge. This confidence in human rationality underpinned his belief that people could peacefully govern themselves through collective deliberation rather than requiring the iron hand of an absolute sovereign.

(2) The State of Nature and Natural Rights

Locke's conception of the state of nature differed from Hobbes's war of all against all. For Locke, the pre-political condition was governed by reason and natural law, which taught that all people, being equal creations of God, have fundamental rights to life, liberty, and property. While this state had inconveniences

- mainly the lack of impartial judges to settle disputes - it was not inherently chaotic or violent.

Importantly, Locke argued that these natural rights exist prior to government and cannot be legitimately surrendered. This concept of inalienable rights would prove enormously influential, particularly in the American Revolution and the Declaration of Independence.

(3) The Two Social Contracts

Locke's innovative contribution is his theory of two distinct social contracts. The first contract creates civil society itself, as individuals agree to live together under common rules and institutions. The second contract establishes specific forms of government to better secure the rights and interests of society's members.

This two-stage theory had crucial implications, as the contract creating civil society remains intact even if a government is dissolved, removing an unjust ruler need not lead to social collapse (as Hobbes had warned). The people retain the right to establish new forms of government while maintaining their social bonds.

(4) Limited Government and the Right of Revolution

Perhaps Locke's most radical conclusion was that political authority must be limited and conditional. Since government's legitimate purpose is protecting natural rights, any ruler who violates these rights or exceeds their proper authority breaks the social contract. In such cases, the people retain a right of revolution - not mere resistance, but the right to remove and replace an unjust government.

This theory provided philosophical justification for the major liberal revolutions that followed: the Glorious Revolution in England (1688), the American Revolution (1776), and even aspects of the French Revolution (1789). Each drew on Locke's ideas about natural rights and the conditional nature of political authority.

(5) The Religious Question

One complexity in Locke's theory is his ambivalent treatment of religion's role in political authority. While explicitly rejecting biblical justifications for government, he frequently referred to God as the author of natural law and human reason. This "taciturnity" on religious foundations reflects both the intellectual climate of his time and perhaps strategic considerations in an era when openly secular political theory remained dangerous.

(6) Legacy and Influence

His ideas shaped the development of liberal democracy, particularly in the Anglo-American tradition. The U.S. Constitution's system of limited government, separation of powers, and protection of individual rights reflects distinctly Lockean principles.

More broadly, Locke's emphasis on reason, natural rights, and the conditional nature of political authority helped establish core principles of modern constitutionalism: that government must be limited, that it derives its authority from the consent of the governed, and that it must respect fundamental human rights. His theory continues to influence debates about democracy, human rights, and the proper limits of governmental power.

3. Development of Capitalism

John Locke's theory of property rights marks a crucial development in the intellectual history of capitalism. Unlike earlier philosophers who viewed property as a secondary concern, Locke placed it at the center of his political theory, arguing that protecting property rights is a fundamental purpose of government.

1) Labor Theory of Property

Locke began with the premise that nature was originally given in common to all humanity. However, he argued that individuals could legitimately convert common resources into private property by mixing their labor with them. This "labor theory of property" suggested that when someone picks an apple or tills unused land, they create a rightful claim to it by adding their labor's value to the natural resource.

This theory has two implications. First, it provided a secular justification for private property based on natural law rather than divine or state authority. Second, it suggested that labor, not just the physical resource itself, creates economic value. Locke argued that human labor could multiply the value of natural resources by "100 or 1000 times," laying philosophical groundwork for later economic theories about wealth creation.

2) Commerce as Civilizing Force

Beyond justifying private property, Locke's theory suggests that commerce itself has a civilizing effect on human society. As later thinkers like Montesquieu and Hirschman would elaborate, the pursuit of economic interest can redirect potentially destructive human passions into productive channels. When people focus on accumulating wealth through trade and industry, they have less inclination toward violence and political tyranny.

3) Political Implications

Locke's ideas profoundly influenced American political thought, particularly through Thomas Jefferson. The notion that government exists primarily to protect property rights (broadly understood to include life, liberty, and physical property) became central to American constitutionalism. However, Locke's theory also acknowledged that different individual capacities could lead to legitimate inequality in property acquisition - a tension that continues to animate debates about capitalism and democracy.

4) Legacy for Market Economics

From Locke's ideas, it is a short hop to market economy and later economic thinkers, particularly Adam Smith. His labor theory of property evolved into Smith's labor theory of value, while his emphasis on individual rights and limited government informed Smith's case for free markets. Though later economists would challenge some of these theoretical foundations, Locke's basic insight – that secure property rights and economic freedom contribute to both prosperity and political liberty – remains influential in modern market economies.

Notably, Locke's theory also acknowledges potential inequality in property acquisition, as different individuals may have different capacities for productive labor. However, he sees this as legitimate so long as it results from varying levels of "industry and rationality" rather than political privilege. This tension between equality of rights and inequality of outcomes remains central to debates about market economies.

By grounding property rights in natural law and human labor rather than state power, Locke provided philosophical foundations for both market economics and constitutional limits on government authority. His theory remains essential for understanding the intellectual origins of modern capitalism and liberal democracy.

CHAPTER VIII. AMERICAN LEGAL TRADITION - THE EARLY YEARS

1. American law and society - A Complex Tapestry of Legal Culture

The American legal system presents a fascinating paradox: while Americans pride themselves on their commitment to the rule of law, their legal history reveals a complex relationship with legal authority that often embraces both adherence to and defiance of established rules. This intricate relationship between law and society in America cannot be understood in isolation but must be examined within its broader social, economic, and historical context.

The American legal system defies simple characterization, being simultaneously complex, contradictory, and deeply intertwined with moral dimensions. This complexity stems partly from the nation's diverse social fabric and its historical development, which has produced a legal culture marked by both reverence for and skepticism toward legal authority.

Historical examples illustrate this paradoxical relationship with law. The American Revolution itself began as what could be characterized as an illegal insurrection against established British rule. The Boston Tea Party, often celebrated in American history, represented a direct challenge to British authority through the destruction of private property. Similarly, the displacement of Native Americans, resulting in the deaths of an estimated 50-80% of the indigenous population since European contact, represents a dark chapter in American legal history where state actions often contradicted fundamental principles of property rights and human dignity.

The tradition of civil disobedience in American society further exemplifies this complex relationship with law. The civil rights movement, for instance, deliberately challenged the "separate but equal" doctrine established by Plessy v. Ferguson (1896), employing tactics ranging from peaceful protest to property destruction. The Prohibition era (1919-1933) demonstrated how widespread noncompliance could ultimately lead to the repeal of a constitutional amendment. Even in contemporary times, controversial issues like abortion rights continue to generate both legal challenges and extra-legal actions.

America's reputation as a litigious society is supported by striking statistics: approximately 100 million cases are filed annually in state courts alone – roughly one case for every two residents. Federal courts process an additional 250,000 cases yearly. With 44 cases filed per 1,000 population, America's litigation rate is comparable to Denmark and England (41 each) and lower than Australia (62), but significantly higher than countries like Germany (23) and Japan (12).

The proliferation of lawyers in American society – approximately one attorney for every 250 people – reflects both the complexity of the legal system and its central role in American life. However, this has also led to criticism regarding frivolous litigation, with numerous examples of seemingly absurd lawsuits making headlines and influencing public perception of the legal system.

Current incarceration statistics present another paradox: with approximately 6.5 million people under some form of correctional supervision (imprisonment, probation, or parole), America's relationship with law enforcement and criminal justice raises important questions about social equity and the effectiveness of legal deterrence.

This complex landscape reveals a distinctive characteristic of American legal culture: the ability to simultaneously maintain respect for the rule of law while preserving space for principled dissent. The legal system operates not merely as a mechanism for maintaining order but as a forum for negotiating social change and expressing moral convictions.

Understanding American law and society requires recognizing this fundamental tension between stability and change, between authority and dissent, and between individual rights and collective welfare. These dynamics continue to shape the evolution of American legal culture, making it a uniquely adaptive yet historically grounded system that reflects the diverse and often contradictory nature of American society itself.

2. Overview of American Legal History in the Early Years

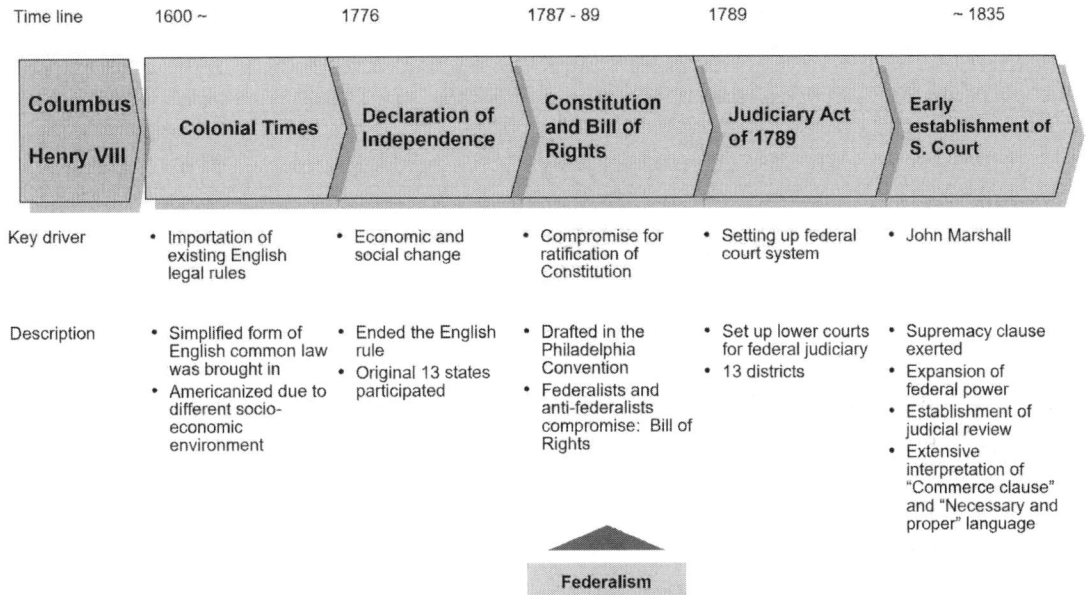

The story of the American legal system begins with the colonial period, where diverse settlements operated under varying degrees of British control. Each colony developed its own legal traditions, influenced by English common law but adapted to local conditions. This diversity would later contribute to the unique federal structure of the United States.

As tensions grew between the colonies and Great Britain, a series of events unfolded that would lead to the American Revolution. The First Continental Congress of 1774 marked a significant step towards united colonial action, setting the stage for the Declaration of Independence in 1776[1]. This pivotal document not only severed ties with England but also articulated fundamental principles of natural rights that would influence American legal thought for generations to come.

The period following independence was marked by experimentation in governance. The Articles of Confederation, ratified in 1781, represented the first attempt at a federal union. However, its weaknesses, particularly the lack of authority granted to the central government, soon became apparent[1]. This led to the Constitutional Convention of 1787, where delegates crafted a new framework for governance that balanced state sovereignty with a stronger federal authority.

The ratification of the Constitution in 1788 and the inauguration of George Washington as the first president in 1789 marked the formal beginning of the United States as we know it today. The Constitution's structure reflected key principles such as separation of powers, checks and balances, and federalism, which continue to shape the American legal landscape.

In the early years of the republic, the legal system faced the challenge of adapting English common law to American conditions while also developing uniquely American legal doctrines. This period saw the rise of important legal figures such as James Kent and Joseph Story, whose treatises played a crucial role in shaping and unifying American law.

The evolution of the American legal system during this formative era set the stage for the complex, dynamic system we see today. It laid the groundwork for the dual federal-state court system, established the principle of judicial review, and began the process of developing distinctly American legal doctrines in areas such as constitutional law, property, and contracts.

3. Constitution and Bill of Rights

1) Dual System of Legal Authority

The American legal system is structured along two fundamental axes: vertical (federalism) and horizontal (separation of powers). The federal arrangement establishes a unique relationship between state and national governments, while the separation of powers distributes authority among three co-equal branches of government.

The Tenth Amendment crystallizes the federal principle by explicitly reserving undelegated powers to the states or the people. States retain general police powers, while federal authority is limited to specifically enumerated powers in the Constitution. This creates a system where states possess residual authority over matters not explicitly assigned to the federal government.

2) Constitutional Development and Ratification

The Constitution, drafted in 1787 following the Articles of Confederation, established a stronger central government with broad Congressional powers and distinct executive and judicial branches. However, concerns about federal overreach led to the Bill of Rights in 1791, which primarily restricted federal, rather than state, authority.

The Bill of Rights emerged from intense debates between Federalists and Anti-Federalists during ratification. These first ten amendments represented a crucial compromise, addressing state concerns about centralized power. The First Amendment, prohibiting establishment of national religion and protecting fundamental freedoms, exemplifies these limitations on federal authority.

3) Early Judicial Framework

The Judiciary Act of 1789 established the federal court system, creating thirteen district courts corresponding to the original states. The Supreme Court's role was initially modest, deciding only 61 cases in its first eleven years—a stark contrast to its current influence in American governance.

This foundation established principles that continue to shape American jurisprudence, balancing state and federal authority while protecting individual rights against government power.

4. Marbury v. Madison (1803) – Establishment of Judicial Review

Background and Facts

In the waning days of John Adams's presidency, William Marbury and several other Federalists received appointments as justices of the peace in the District of Columbia. These appointments, though approved by Congress and signed by Adams, were never fully executed before Thomas Jefferson took office. When Jefferson's administration refused to honor these "midnight appointments," Marbury and his fellow appointees sought legal remedy directly from the Supreme Court under the Judiciary Act of 1789.

Legal Questions Presented

The Court faced three distinct questions: First, whether Marbury had a legitimate right to his appointment; second, whether the law provided a remedy for such a denial of rights; and third, whether the Supreme Court possessed the proper jurisdiction to issue a writ of mandamus compelling the delivery of his commission.

Court's Analysis and Holding

Chief Justice Marshall, writing for the Court, methodically addressed each question. The Court determined that Marbury did indeed have a right to his commission and that the law should provide a remedy for such a violation. However, on the crucial third question, Marshall concluded that while the Judiciary Act of 1789 purported to give the Supreme Court original jurisdiction over writs of mandamus, this grant of power exceeded the scope of jurisdiction defined in Article III of the Constitution.

Significance and Impact

The true significance of Marbury v. Madison, 5 U.S. 137 (1803) lies not in its resolution of Marbury's appointment but in Marshall's assertion of judicial review. By declaring that "an act of the legislature repugnant to the constitution is void," the Court established its fundamental power to review the constitutionality of legislative acts. This principle of judicial review, though not explicitly stated in the Constitution, became a cornerstone of American constitutional law, establishing the Supreme Court as the ultimate arbiter of constitutional interpretation.

5. Marshall Court and Federalism

1) John Marshall, the 4th Chief Justice of the Supreme Court of the U.S.

John Marshall's extraordinary thirty-four-year tenure as Chief Justice (1801-1835) profoundly shaped American jurisprudence. As the fourth Chief Justice of the Supreme Court, Marshall transformed the judicial branch from a relatively weak institution into a co-equal branch of government, establishing precedents that continue to influence constitutional interpretation today.

Marshall's most enduring contribution was the establishment of judicial review, articulated in the landmark case Marbury v. Madison. This doctrine empowered courts to declare laws unconstitutional, effectively positioning the judiciary as the ultimate interpreter of the Constitution. This fundamental principle transformed the Supreme Court from a potentially subordinate institution into a powerful check on both executive and legislative authority.

Marshall consistently advanced a strong federalist vision, strengthening national authority through a series of pivotal decisions. His expansive interpretation of enumerated powers, particularly regarding federal supremacy over state law, created a robust framework for national governance. This approach established clear hierarchies of legal authority while maintaining sufficient flexibility for the federal system to evolve with the growing nation.

Through these contributions, Marshall effectively laid the groundwork for modern American constitutional law, establishing principles that would guide judicial interpretation for centuries to come. His vision of a strong federal judiciary capable of enforcing constitutional limits on government power remains a cornerstone of American democracy.

2) The Marshall Court's Transformation of American Federalism

(1) Judicial Supremacy

Chief Justice Marshall fundamentally reshaped American governance through Marbury v. Madison, establishing the federal courts, particularly the Supreme Court, as authoritative interpreters of constitutional law. This doctrine of judicial review transformed the Court from a relatively weak institution into a powerful arbiter of governmental policy.

(2) National Supremacy

Marshall vigorously defended federal supremacy against state resistance, even when states challenged the Supreme Court's appellate jurisdiction over their highest courts. He argued that allowing states to independently interpret federal law would fragment legal consistency and effectively create sovereign states. The Supremacy Clause of Article VI provided constitutional foundation for this position, declaring federal law the "Supreme Law of the land." This principle was tested when Virginia challenged the Supreme Court's appellate jurisdiction in a case involving District of Columbia lottery tickets. Cohens v. Virginia, 19 U.S. 264 (1821). Marshall affirmed the Court's jurisdiction, though ultimately ruling against the lottery operators, demonstrating that federal supremacy did not automatically favor federal interests.

Staunch Federalist, Marshall systematically broadened federal authority through three key areas of commerce clause, necessary and proper clause.

(3) Broad Interpretation of Commerce Clause

In Gibbons v. Ogden, Marshall expansively interpreted the Commerce Clause, invalidating New York's steamboat monopoly as inconsistent with federal regulation of interstate commerce. This landmark decision established a broad understanding of commerce that included navigation and defined "among the several states" to grant Congress substantial regulatory authority.

(4) Expansive Application of Necessary and Proper Clause

McCulloch v. Maryland further expanded federal power by broadly interpreting the Necessary and Proper Clause. Marshall upheld Congress's authority to establish a national bank and protected it from state taxation, articulating a doctrine of implied powers that significantly strengthened federal authority.

""

CHAPTER IX. AMERICAN JUDICIAL SYSTEM

1. Sources and Types of American Law

1) Sources of Legal Authority

The American legal system draws from multiple sources of authority, arranged in a complex hierarchy. At the apex stands the Constitution, the supreme law of the land. Below this foundational document, legislative bodies at various levels of government create statutory law. These include Congress at the federal level, state legislatures, county commissioners, city councils, and thousands of special districts that oversee specific functions like education, fire prevention, and municipal utilities.

Another significant source comes from quasi-legislative and quasi-judicial bodies. These administrative entities—including federal agencies like the Securities and Exchange Commission (SEC), state boards, and local authorities—make important regulatory decisions that carry the force of law. Political executives also contribute to the legal framework through mechanisms like presidential executive orders and emergency declarations by state governors.

2) Classifications of Law

The American legal system can be categorized in several ways. One traditional division separates statutory law (enacted by legislatures) from common law (developed through court decisions). Another distinguishes between civil law, which resolves disputes between parties, and criminal law, which addresses offenses against society. Equity law provides remedies when traditional legal solutions prove inadequate.

The system also differentiates between private law governing relationships between individuals and public law, which includes constitutional, administrative, and other governmental matters. Finally, the federal structure of American government creates parallel systems of state and federal law, each with its own jurisdiction and authority. Finally, the laws could be state or federal as the Fig. 6 shows.

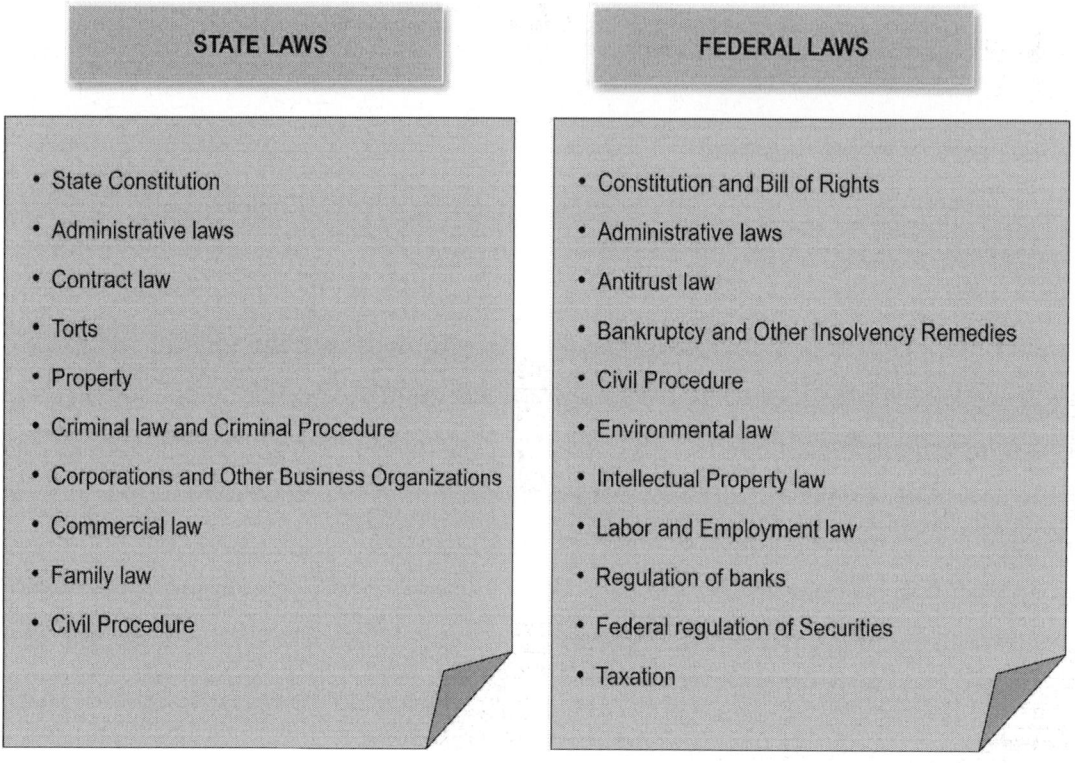

Fig. 6.

2. The Federal Court System

1) Historical Development

The structure of the federal judiciary emerged from intense debates during the Constitutional Convention. The Virginia Plan advocated for a comprehensive federal court system with both Supreme Court and lower courts, while the New Jersey Plan proposed only a Supreme Court. The compromise was reflected in Article III of the Constitution, which established "one supreme Court" while leaving the creation of "inferior Courts" to Congressional discretion.

When the First Congress convened in 1789, establishing a national court system became an immediate priority. The resulting Judiciary Act of 1789 created a three-tiered system: the Supreme Court with a Chief Justice and five Associate Justices, three circuit courts staffed by Supreme Court Justices and district judges, and thirteen district courts. Notably, the Supreme Court's early years were quiet—it decided no cases in its first three years and only about fifty cases in its first decade.

2) Evolution of the Federal Courts

The federal court system continued to evolve throughout the 19th and early 20th centuries. The Evarts Act of 1891 established the circuit courts of appeals, creating a four-court structure with two trial courts (district and circuit) and two appellate courts. In 1911, Congress abolished the old circuit courts, streamlining the system. A significant development occurred in 1925 when Congress granted the Supreme Court discretionary review through the writ of certiorari, allowing it to select which cases to hear. Today, the Court typically issues full decisions in only 80-90 cases annually.

3) Contemporary Structure and Jurisdiction

The modern federal court system consists of three main tiers. District courts serve as the primary trial courts, with multiple districts in larger states like California, New York, and Texas. The Courts of Appeals, organized into eleven geographical circuits, handle appeals from district courts and review for legal (not factual) errors. The Supreme Court, located in Washington, D.C., possesses both original jurisdiction (primarily in cases between states) and appellate jurisdiction, functioning as both a court of last resort and a significant policy-making institution through constitutional interpretation.

4) Specialized Courts

Alongside these Article III courts, Congress has established specialized "legislative courts" under Article I, Section 8. These include military courts, bankruptcy courts, and the Foreign Intelligence Surveillance Court (established in 1978 and expanded under the USA PATRIOT Act). These courts help administer specific Congressional statutes and often combine administrative, quasi-legislative, and judicial functions.

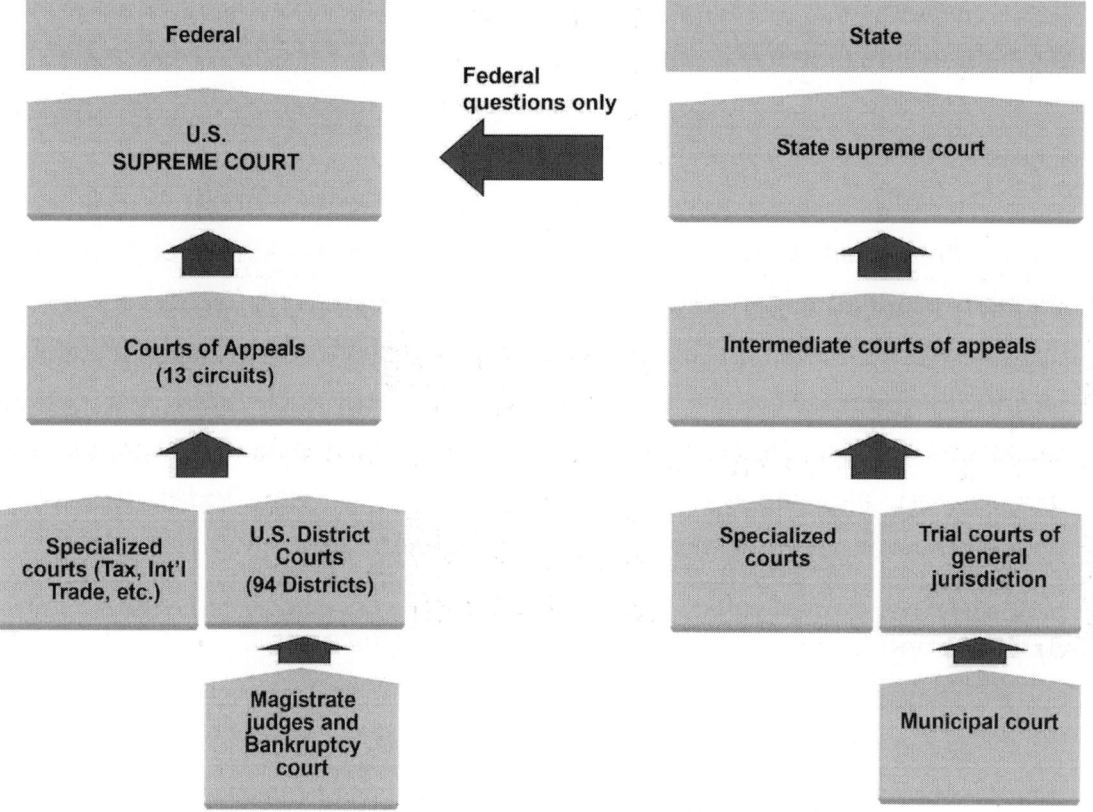

Fig. 7. Courts and the Appeals Routes

3. State Court System

1) Historical Development

State courts predate the federal judiciary, originating in colonial times when states functioned as sovereign entities with their own constitutions. During the colonial period, governors appointed by the English crown wielded consolidated executive, legislative, and judicial powers. The colonial judicial system was relatively simple, consisting of three tiers: local justices of the peace or magistrates at the lowest level, county courts as general trial courts, and the governor's council as the highest court.

By the early 18th century, increasing commercial activity and property disputes, coupled with the arrival of English-trained lawyers, prompted the development of a more sophisticated court system. Between 1760 and 1820, state courts increasingly aligned with English common law principles. Though the American Revolution didn't necessitate a complete overhaul, the courts gradually gained independence as conflicts with legislative bodies multiplied.

2) Post-Civil War Evolution

The post-Civil War era saw significant changes in state court systems. Rapid societal development and diverse legal needs led to the creation of specialized courts with varying jurisdictions. This proliferation resulted in what scholars term "fragmentation"—a confusing patchwork of courts lacking consistency across states. While the court unification movement attempted to address this problem, resistance from entrenched interests, particularly local judges and lawyers, has hampered comprehensive reform.

3) Modern Organization

Contemporary state court systems exhibit considerable diversity in structure and nomenclature. Most states organize their courts into municipal courts and superior courts at the trial level, with municipal courts handling about 85% of all cases. These limited-jurisdiction courts manage matters such as traffic violations, domestic relations, misdemeanors, and small claims under $1,000. Superior courts serve as courts of general jurisdiction, operating within defined judicial districts or circuits.

Forty states maintain intermediate appellate courts, a significant increase from just thirteen in 1911. Every state has a court of last resort (typically called the Supreme Court), with Oklahoma and Texas uniquely maintaining separate highest courts for civil and criminal matters. Additionally, specialized courts, such as juvenile courts, handle specific types of cases.

4) Contemporary Functions

State courts serve dual functions in the American legal system. Lower courts focus primarily on norm enforcement, handling day-to-day legal matters and ensuring compliance with state laws. Meanwhile, appellate and highest courts engage in significant policy-making through their interpretations of state constitutions and laws, paralleling the federal judiciary's role in shaping American law and society.

4. Stare Decisis: Stability and Evolution in Common Law

1) The Dual Nature of Common Law

The common law system exhibits a fascinating duality in its approach to precedent. Through stare decisis, it maintains a conservative adherence to past decisions, providing stability and predictability. Simultaneously, it demonstrates remarkable adaptability through judicial interpretation, allowing for organic evolution of legal principles to meet changing societal needs.

2) The Art of Extracting Legal Principles

The challenge of deriving broader principles from specific cases is illustrated by the famous "snail in the bottle" case. Suppose a man bought his companion a lemonade contained in an opaque bottle. When she had poured most of the liquid into a glass and drunk some of it, the woman discovered the decomposing remains of a snail at the bottom of the bottle. She became very ill and sued the manufacturer of the lemonade. She won the case in the appellate level. What is the holding though?
- Manufacturer of lemonade in opaque bottle is liable to people who become ill after drinking the beverage and then discovering a decomposing snail inside the bottle. – this would be absurdly specific

- All manufacturers of goods are liable to any person who is injured by defects in the product. – this would be too broad

The skill of common law reasoning lies in finding the appropriate middle ground that establishes meaningful precedent while maintaining flexibility for future application.

3) Beyond Individual Cases

As stated in "Fundamentals of American Law," individual cases are not viewed as final, definitive statements of law. Rather, the common law operates through the accumulation of cases, with courts extracting and refining legal principles over time. This process, as Lord Mansfield notably observed, allows the common law to "work itself pure from case to case."

4) Common Law as Social Mirror

The evolutionary nature of common law enables it to reflect and respond to societal changes. Through careful interpretation and application of precedent, courts can maintain legal stability while adapting to new social realities. This balance between consistency and flexibility distinguishes common law as a uniquely responsive legal system.

The principle of stare decisis thus serves not as a rigid constraint but as a framework for guided legal evolution, allowing courts to honor precedent while ensuring the law remains relevant to contemporary society.

5. Common Law Legal Reasoning

Form of Legal Reasoning: What do lawyers really do when they write an office memo or trial brief? There are some basic types of reasoning they'll use to try to persuade a judge or jury

1) Rule-based reasoning

When you use *rule-based reasoning*, you must first figure out just what the rule is. If the rule is a statute, for example, it will be easy to pick out. It's harder to pick out the rule from case law. Once you know the rule, you can use the rule to solve the problem at hand. In a predictive memo you say: "If you do *this*, then based on *these* authorities *this* will probably happen."

2) Analogical Reasoning

Analogical reasoning is something we've done all our lives. You look for similarities between the authorities and the case at hand. You say: "The facts of this case are like the facts of the case where the rule comes from." Notice how this is similar to rule-based reasoning.

3) Counter-analogical reasoning

Counter-analogical reasoning is just the opposite. You point out the differences between the facts of the case at hand and the facts the case where the rule comes from. This is something you will want to do if the rule is bad for your client. You say: "Sure, that was the rule in that case, and if it were applied to this case I would lose. But this case isn't like that case." This is what we do when we say that a certain case or hypothetical is *distinguishable* from an authoritative case.

4) Policy-based reasoning

Policy-based reasoning goes along with counter-analogical reasoning. "Say the rule is X. Let's also say that the rule was created to eliminate behavior Y. But what we have in the present case is behavior Z, which is not the behavior we were trying to prevent. In fact, it might be behavior society wants to encourage. Therefore, we should not enforce rule X in the case of behavior Z." e.g., Safety belt legislation

5) Narrative reasoning

Narrative reasoning is frequently seen in closing arguments on TV trials. You persuade the listener by telling a story in a compelling way so that your story has a gut appeal. You have the chance to color your case and client with whatever characteristics they have which are most appealing or favorable. Take *Hawkins v. McGee* for example: you could spin the story to make the grafting doctor a right bastard. But that doesn't have much to do with a particular rule of law. But it does have persuasive value. The doctor has encouraged activity that turns out to be harmful to someone else.

CHAPTER X. DISPUTE RESOLUTION – TRIAL

1. Case Studies

1) The McDonald's Hot Coffee Case, Liebeck v. McDonald's (1994)

(1) Facts of the Case **Trial as a looking glass into the judicial system:**

In 1992, Stella Liebeck, a 79-year-old woman, suffered third-degree burns when McDonald's coffee spilled on her lap while she was a passenger in her grandson's parked car. The coffee was served at 180-190°F (82-88°C), significantly hotter than coffee typically served at home (135-140°F or 57-60°C). The burns were severe enough to require skin grafts and an eight-day hospital stay.

(2) Arguments

Liebeck initially sought only $20,000 to cover her medical expenses, but McDonald's offered just $800. Later settlement attempts, including a mediator's suggestion of $225,000, were rejected by McDonald's. The plaintiff's attorneys argued that McDonald's coffee was "dangerously hot," pointing to over 700 previous burn incidents reported to the company. They contended that coffee at 180-190°F would cause third-degree burns in about 3 seconds, while coffee at 160°F would allow 12-15 seconds for preventive action.

McDonald's defended its practice, arguing that customers wanted their coffee hot enough to stay warm during their commute or drive to work. They maintained that their coffee temperature was industry standard and that customers were aware of potential risks.

(3) Outcome of the case

The jury awarded Liebeck $200,000 in compensatory damages (reduced to $160,000 due to 20% comparative negligence) and $2.7 million in punitive damages (later reduced to $480,000 by the trial judge). The case ultimately settled for an undisclosed amount before appeal.

(4) Impact and Implications

This case became a symbol of frivolous litigation in the American legal system, though many legal scholars argue this characterization is unfair. McDonalds was on notice of the danger as 700 similar cases had been filed against the company. This willful disregard of the known danger, as can be argued, might have angered the jury to elect to "send a strong message" to the company.

The case led to significant changes in how companies handle product safety and warning labels. It also sparked debates about tort reform and punitive damages in American civil litigation. McDonald's and other restaurants now serve coffee at lower temperatures and include more explicit warnings. The case demonstrates how civil litigation can force corporate policy changes and highlights the role of punitive damages in deterring corporate misconduct. It remains a landmark example of how the American civil justice system can compel large corporations to prioritize consumer safety over operational convenience.

2). Examples of punitive damages: Signaling and Judicial Oversight.

Punitive damages serve as a powerful mechanism in the American legal system to signal societal disapproval of egregious corporate behavior while providing courts with tools to moderate excessive jury awards. Two notable examples illustrate this dual function.

(1) The Signaling Function

The landmark case of Erin Brockovich v. Pacific Gas & Electric resulted in a $333 million verdict in 1996, the largest direct lawsuit settlement at the time. This case demonstrated how punitive damages could force corporations to address environmental contamination and public health concerns. More dramatically, tobacco litigation in the early 2000s produced unprecedented punitive damage awards. In 2000, a Florida jury awarded $145 billion in punitive damages against the nation's five largest tobacco companies—the largest monetary penalty in U.S. history at that time. Philip Morris alone was assessed $73.9 billion in damages.

Subsequent tobacco litigation continued to produce significant verdicts: a $15 million award in Kansas (2002), $37.5 million in Miami for a single plaintiff who lost his tongue to cancer, and a stunning $28 billion verdict against Philip Morris in Los Angeles (later reduced to $28 million). In 2004, a groundbreaking New York case awarded $20 million to a widow, marking the first time a New York court held a tobacco company liable for an individual smoker's death.

(2) Judicial Oversight

However, the legal system includes safeguards against excessive punitive damages through procedures like Judgment Notwithstanding the Verdict (JNOV). This allows judges to modify or overturn jury verdicts they find unreasonable or unsupported by evidence. The dramatic reduction of the Los Angeles verdict against Philip Morris from $28 billion to $28 million exemplifies this moderating function. Judges effectively ask, "Has the jury lost perspective?" and can adjust awards to maintain proportionality between the punishment and the offense.

This balance between allowing juries to signal society's disapproval through large punitive awards while providing judicial oversight to ensure reasonableness has become a hallmark of American civil litigation, particularly in cases involving corporate misconduct affecting public health and safety.

2. Judicial Procedure Before Trial

The pre-trial phase of litigation in the United States is a crucial stage that sets the foundation for the eventual trial or settlement of a case. This phase encompasses several key processes designed to define the issues, gather evidence, and prepare the parties for trial.

1) Commencement of Action

The initiation of legal proceedings differs significantly between civil and criminal cases. In civil litigation, the process begins when a plaintiff files a complaint with the court, outlining their grievances and the relief sought. The court then issues a summons, which, along with the complaint, must be served on the defendant, notifying them of the action and requiring a response.

In contrast, criminal proceedings are typically initiated by the government. The process often begins with an arrest or a grand jury indictment, depending on the jurisdiction and the severity of the alleged crime. Following arrest, the accused is brought before a judge for an initial appearance, where they are informed of the charges and their rights. In more serious cases, a preliminary hearing or grand jury proceeding may follow to determine if there is probable cause to proceed with the case.

2) Pleadings

Pleadings are formal written statements exchanged between the parties that outline their respective positions. In the U.S. legal system, the pleading practice requires parties to state all possible causes of action and defenses. This approach, known as "notice pleading," aims to give fair notice of the claims and defenses to all parties involved.

The plaintiff's complaint is followed by the defendant's answer, which may include denials of the plaintiff's allegations, affirmative defenses, counterclaims against the plaintiff, cross-claims against co-defendants, and third-party claims against non-parties.

Suppose there is a dog-bite case. Pleadings could assert:
- Complaint: Your dog bit me. I am suing for damages
- Defense: My dog didn't bite you, My dog is real friendly, My dog might have bitten you but you were not hurt, and by the way, I don't have a dog
- Another formulation: It didn't happen, We didn't do it, Somebody else did it, You weren't hurt, You weren't hurt as bad as you say you were, and besides you weren't there

This example illustrates the variety of defenses a defendant might raise, from outright denial to alternative explanations and mitigating factors.

3) Discovery

Discovery is a critical pre-trial process that allows parties to obtain information from each other and third parties. The primary methods of discovery include interrogatories, depositions, requests for production of documents, inspections, and requests for admissions, but legal strategies are not discoverable. The goal of discovery is to prevent surprise at trial and to allow both sides to fully prepare their cases.

Discovery in civil litigation must adhere to relevancy standard established by the Federal Rules of Civil Procedure (FRCP). Information sought through discovery must be "reasonably calculated to lead to the discovery of admissible evidence." This requirement serves as a fundamental limitation, preventing what courts often term "fishing expeditions".

Several procedural safeguards restrict the scope of discovery. For instance, parties cannot use discovery tools to probe opposing counsel's legal strategy, as this would violate attorney work product privilege. Geographic limitations also apply: nonparty witnesses cannot be compelled to travel more than 100 miles from their residence for depositions. Furthermore, depositions may not be used against any party who did not receive proper notice of the deposition process.

Under FRCP 26(b), courts maintain considerable discretion in managing discovery. Certain categories receive special treatment. For example, insurance agreements relevant to the case are generally discoverable, while materials prepared in anticipation of trial receive qualified protection. Expert witness discovery follows specific protocols designed to balance the need for information with the protection of expert work product.

Privileged communications represent a crucial exception to discovery requirements. Three primary privileges protect confidential communications: attorney-client, doctor-patient, and marital privileges. The scope of marital privilege varies by jurisdiction, particularly regarding timing - some courts protect only communications after marriage, others only before divorce, and some jurisdictions protect communications during the entire marriage period.

The work product doctrine provides additional protection for attorneys' case preparation materials. This doctrine shields mental impressions, conclusions, opinions, and legal theories developed in anticipation of litigation. This protection ensures attorneys can prepare cases thoroughly without fear their strategic thinking will be exposed to opposing counsel through discovery.

4) Pre-trial Motions

Pre-trial motions are formal requests made to the court to resolve various issues before the trial begins. A motion to dismiss challenges the legal sufficiency of the complaint, arguing that even if all the facts alleged are true, they do not constitute a valid legal claim. A motion for summary judgment contends that there is no genuine dispute about any material fact and that the moving party is entitled to judgment as a matter of law. Motions in limine are used to request that certain evidence be excluded from trial, often on the grounds that it is irrelevant, prejudicial, or otherwise inadmissible.

5) Pre-trial Conferences

Pre-trial conferences are meetings between the judge and the parties' attorneys to discuss the management of the case. These conferences serve to narrow the issues for trial, facilitate settlement discussions, and establish schedules for further proceedings. They also provide an opportunity to address evidentiary issues and determine the expected length of the trial. Judges may use these conferences to encourage parties to consider alternative dispute resolution methods or to explore the possibility of settlement. By clarifying the issues and procedures in advance, pre-trial conferences can significantly streamline the trial process and often lead to resolutions without the need for a full trial.

3. Trial

1) Overview of a Trial

Greek rhetorics has a theory that in order to persuade listeners, you tell the story three times: You tell them what story you are going to tell, tell the story, and then tell them what you told. Trials fundamentally operate in a similar fashion, opening statement, presentation of evidence and closing argument corresponding to the thrice told stories. Jurors are the listeners.

THE ART OF PERSUASION IN TRIAL ADVOCACY: ANCIENT WISDOM IN MODERN COURTS

The structure of modern trials reflects an ancient principle of persuasion developed by Greek rhetoricians. They posited that effective communication requires telling a story three times: Tell them what you are going to tell them, Tell them the story itself, and Tell them what you story told them. This three-part structure maximizes comprehension and retention while reinforcing key messages.

Modern trial procedure follows this classical framework remarkably closely, as the Fig below shows. The opening statement, presentation of evidence, and the closing argument, serving as the thrice told story.

This parallel is more than coincidental - it reflects a fundamental understanding of how humans process and retain information. With jurors serving as the critical audience, this structure helps them comprehend complex facts and arguments, ultimately enabling them to reach reasoned verdicts based on the evidence presented.

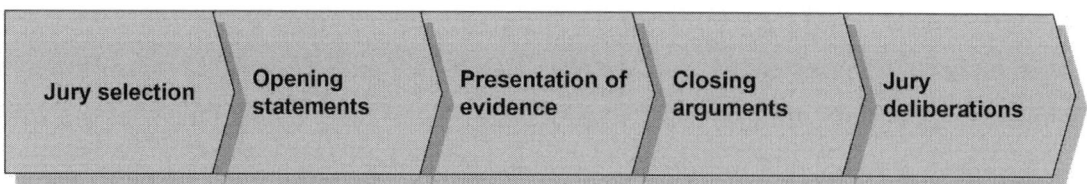

Fig 8. Anatomy of a trial: from jury selection to verdict

2) Jury Selection

The trial process begins with voir dire, where attorneys and the judge question potential jurors to form an impartial panel. This critical phase allows counsel to identify and excuse jurors who might struggle to render an unbiased verdict due to personal beliefs, experiences, or prejudices. Through this careful screening process, both parties work to ensure the constitutional right to a fair trial by an impartial jury.

3) Opening Statements

Following jury selection, attorneys present their opening statements, offering a roadmap of their case to the jury. These statements outline the anticipated evidence and what each side intends to prove. While compelling, opening statements do not constitute evidence, as attorneys are not considered witnesses. Since lawyers cannot testify and evidence has not been admitted, attorneys use "Evidence will show…" as preface to their statements. By convention, the plaintiff's attorney in civil cases or the prosecutor in criminal cases presents first, setting the stage for the trial.

4) Presentation of Evidence

The evidentiary phase begins with the plaintiff's or prosecutor's witnesses testifying under oath. Each witness undergoes direct examination by the calling attorney, followed by cross-examination from opposing counsel. This adversarial process aims to elicit truthful testimony and establish facts. During this phase, attorneys may also introduce physical evidence and exhibits to support their cases. The formal rules of evidence govern all testimony and exhibits presented.

Moving party has the burden of proof: "beyond the reasonable doubt" in a criminal case, and "Preponderance of evidence" in a civil case.

(1) Direct examination

Direct examination is a phase of trial where attorneys elicit testimony to present their case narrative to the jury. Its primary purpose is to tell a convincing story through evidence while allowing jurors to experience events from the presenting side's perspective. The effectiveness depends largely on witness testimony, evaluated through the witness's background, content of testimony, and demeanor. While testimony is the main tool, attorneys may also utilize exhibits, computer simulations, and video evidence. Witnesses may be lay persons, experts, character witnesses, or adverse parties, each requiring different examination approaches.

(2) Cross examination

Cross-examination serves as the adversarial counterpoint to direct examination, designed to test and challenge the credibility of witness testimony. Its fundamental purpose is twofold: to elicit testimony favorable to the cross-examiner's case and to diminish the impact of harmful testimony from direct examination. This phase provides the opportunity to expose inconsistencies, bias, or gaps in the witness's testimony.

Attorneys typically employ leading questions during cross-examination, maintaining tight control over witness responses. The traditional approach follows the "chapter method," where each topic is addressed separately and conclusively

before moving to the next. Effective cross-examination often builds toward key admissions through a series of short, carefully crafted questions that demand simple "yes" or "no" answers. Successful cross-examination adheres to several cardinal rules:
- Never ask a question without knowing the answer
- Keep questions brief and focused
- Limit each question to a single fact
- Stop when the point is made
- Avoid repeating favorable direct testimony
- Save critical points for closing argument

These principles, while not absolute, provide a framework for controlling hostile witnesses while advancing the cross-examiner's theory of the case.

(3) Rules of evidence

The rules of evidence govern what information can be presented and how it may be introduced during trial proceedings. Evidence generally falls into three main categories: real evidence (physical objects), testimony from witnesses, and expert witness testimony governed by Federal Rule of Civil Procedure 702. Evidence may be either direct, providing immediate proof of a fact, or circumstantial, requiring inference to establish a fact.

The presentation of evidence follows a structured process through direct examination, cross-examination, and redirect examination. During direct examination, witness credibility is paramount. Cross-examination permits leading questions to challenge testimony, while redirect examination offers an opportunity to rehabilitate witnesses whose credibility may have been damaged during cross-examination.

(4) Objections and the Admissibility Test

The foundation of evidentiary objections rests on three fundamental principles: relevancy, materiality, and competency. Together, these form the basic admissibility test that all evidence must pass. Evidence must first be relevant, having some probative value to the case at hand. Second, it must be material, bearing directly on the decision of the case. Third, it must be competent, satisfying rules of admissibility such as the best evidence rule.

Beyond these foundational objections, attorneys may raise procedural challenges to questioning techniques. These include objections to misleading questions that force specific answers, confusing questions that are overly rapid or redundant, and improperly constructed questions using compound sentences. Additionally, attorneys may object to argumentative questioning that badgers witnesses or expresses counsel's personal opinions, premature introduction of evidence before proper foundation, and conclusionary questions that call for hearsay testimony.

Each objection serves as a crucial tool for maintaining the integrity of trial proceedings and ensuring that jurors receive only proper evidence for consideration.

(5) Hearsay

Hearsay refers to "second-hand" testimony where a witness reports statements made by others rather than their direct observations. The rule against hearsay, rooted in the infamous 1603 trial of Sir Walter Raleigh, who was wrongfully convicted of treason based on layered hearsay testimony (testimony that someone had overheard someone else say they heard Sir Raleigh would slit the King's throat), reflects fundamental concerns about reliability and the constitutional right to confront accusers under the Sixth Amendment.

However, practical necessity has led to five major exceptions to the hearsay rule: dying declarations, spontaneous or excited utterances, present sense impressions, admissions against interest, and business or public records. These exceptions are based on circumstances that provide inherent reliability or necessity that outweigh the general concerns about hearsay evidence. The law presumes that statements made under these conditions carry sufficient indicia of reliability to warrant admission despite their hearsay nature.

5) Closing Arguments

Closing arguments represent each side's final opportunity to address the jury. The plaintiff's attorney presents first, analyzing the evidence presented and arguing how it supports their case. The defense follows with their interpretation of the evidence and counter-arguments. Both sides may have rebuttal opportunities to address specific points raised by opposing counsel. These arguments synthesize the evidence and attempt to persuade jurors to reach a favorable verdict.

6) Jury Deliberations

The final phase begins with the judge's instructions on applicable law. Jurors then retire to deliberate in complete privacy, discussing the evidence and attempting to reach a verdict. Once they reach a decision, they select a foreperson to communicate their verdict to the court. The verdict is then read aloud in open court, bringing the trial to its conclusion.

(1) Right of trial by jury – a historical note

The right to trial by jury emerged in England as a crucial check against centralized royal power. First codified in the Magna Carta of 1215, this right represented a significant limitation on monarchical authority. The charter's famous provision that no freeman shall be condemned except "by lawful judgment of his peers" established jury trial as a fundamental safeguard of individual liberty against arbitrary state power.

The American Constitution embraced and expanded this tradition, mentioning jury trials in three distinct provisions. Article III, Section 2 mandates jury trials for all federal criminal cases except impeachment. The Sixth Amendment guarantees criminal defendants the right to a "speedy and public trial, by an impartial jury," a protection later extended to state courts through the Fourteenth Amendment's due process clause. The Seventh Amendment preserves jury trials for civil cases involving more than twenty dollars, though this provision notably has not been incorporated against the states.

The Supreme Court has consistently reinforced the importance of jury trials through landmark decisions. Sheppard v. Maxwell (1966) protected against prejudicial publicity, while Duncan v. Louisiana (1968) extended constitutional jury protections to state courts. In Williams v. Florida (1970), the Court articulated the jury's essential role as a safeguard against prosecutorial overreach and judicial bias, highlighting its continued significance in the American justice system.

(2) American jury system

The right to a jury trial in criminal cases applies only to adults charged with serious offenses—excluding juvenile cases and minor misdemeanors carrying sentences less than six months. In civil matters, states maintain discretion in determining which disputes warrant jury trials, as the Seventh Amendment's civil jury provision has never been incorporated against the states.

Jury size varies between federal and state courts. While England established the twelve-person jury in the 14th century, American courts have adopted more flexible approaches. Federal criminal trials require twelve jurors, but state courts may use six-person juries. Both federal and state courts permit six-person juries in civil cases.

Unanimity requirements also differ across jurisdictions. Federal criminal trials demand unanimous verdicts, following English tradition. Since April 2020, in the case of Ramos v. Louisiana, the Supreme Court ruled that unanimous jury verdicts are required for serious criminal cases in all states, overturning previous precedents that allowed split jury verdicts.

4. Appeals Process

The appellate process serves as a mechanism for error correction and legal development in American jurisprudence. At its core, appellate review involves multiple judges examining a trial court's decision in a detached setting, embodying the principle that "several heads are better than one." Typically, three-judge panels hear appeals, though significant cases may warrant "En Banc" sessions that usually involve the entire court.

The dual purpose of appellate review encompasses both error correction and policy formulation. In its error-correction role, appellate courts protect litigants from arbitrary, capricious, or mistaken decisions by trial judges. Additionally, appellate courts serve a vital law-making function, shaping legal doctrine in response to evolving societal conditions through published opinions that promote uniformity within their jurisdiction.

However, appellate review operates within strict parameters. Courts may only consider questions of law properly raised at trial, and generally only final judgments are appealable, with limited exceptions for interlocutory appeals. While losing parties typically have discretion to appeal, prosecutors cannot appeal not-guilty verdicts due to double jeopardy protections. Death penalty cases uniquely require mandatory appeal. The prohibition against double jeopardy prevents second prosecutions for the same crime by the same sovereign after a final verdict, reinforcing the finality of criminal proceedings.

The diagram (Fig. 8) shows a general procedure for appellate process, state and federal, but procedural requirements for written brief and filing dates, etc. could vary depending on the states. Generally, federal appellate courts have more strict procedural requirements.

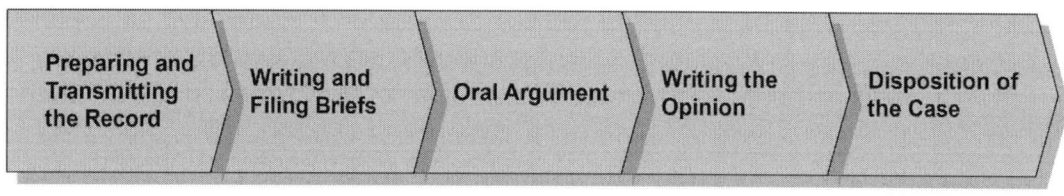

- After the appellant files a notice of appeal within the prescribed time after the trial, the appellate court records are forwarded to the appeals court
  – Case file along with transcripts of the testimony
- A brief is a written argument that sets forth the party's view of the facts of the case, the issues raised in the appeal, and the precedents supporting the party's position
- Lawyers on both sides are given a limited time to argue for their respective position
- After the argument, the court recesses to engage in the group deliberation
- One judge in the majority is assigned to write the opinion
- Dissenting opinion may be also attached
- The court disposes the case by either affirm, modify, or reverse the previous decision
- Also, the court may remand the case to the lower court for further proceedings

Fig. 8. Appellate process overview

CHAPTER XI. SUPREME COURT OF THE UNINTED STATES REVISITED

1. Overview

The Supreme Court is both the highest appellate court and guardian of constitutional supremacy. Composed of a Chief Justice and eight Associate Justices appointed by the President with Senate confirmation, the Court's members serve life terms "during good behavior," ensuring judicial independence from political pressures.

The Court's primary functions encompass three key areas. First, it maintains constitutional supremacy by safeguarding federalism, enforcing separation of powers, and protecting individual rights. Second, it ensures uniform application of federal law across all jurisdictions. Third, it resolves disputes between states in its limited original jurisdiction capacity.

Beyond these formal roles, the Court's significance stems from its position as an institutional pillar in American governance. Through the doctrine of stare decisis (adherence to precedent), it shapes law by establishing binding interpretations of constitutional and statutory provisions. Perhaps most notably, the Court serves as a powerful agent of social change through its policy-making function, particularly in areas involving civil rights and individual liberties.

Meeting in Washington, D.C., the Court selectively chooses its cases, focusing on issues of national importance that require constitutional interpretation or resolution of conflicts between lower courts.

2. Jurisdiction of SCOTUS

1) Original jurisdiction

The Supreme Court's jurisdiction encompasses both original and appellate authority. Under Article III, the Court maintains original jurisdiction over cases involving ambassadors, public ministers, consuls, and disputes between states. In these rare instances, the Court functions as a trial court, though it now typically delegates fact-finding to Special Masters.

2) Appellate jurisdiction

The Court's appellate jurisdiction derives from three sources. First, statutory appeals from lower court decisions declaring laws unconstitutional, though technically mandatory, are handled discretionarily in practice. Second, and most significantly, the Court exercises discretionary review through writs of certiorari, allowing it to select cases of particular importance. While the Court focused on economic and federalism issues in the 1930s-40s, today's docket predominantly features cases involving due process, civil liberties, and equality. Third, certification allows appellate courts to request clarification on points of federal law, though this mechanism is rarely used.

3) Certiorari system of case selection for review

The Court's selectivity is evident in its statistics: of approximately 6,000- 8,000 annual petitions, only 70-80 cases receive full review. Nearly 90% of petitions are denied or dismissed, while about 10% receive summary disposition. This careful case selection ensures the Court focuses its attention on the most significant legal issues facing the nation.

3. Composition of the Court

The current Supreme Court consists of nine Justices, with six conservatives (Roberts, Thomas, Alito, Gorsuch, Kavanaugh, and Barrett) and three liberals (Sotomayor, Kagan, and Jackson). Most Justices attended either Harvard or Yale Law School, reflecting a remarkably narrow educational background. The Court's composition has historically included informal "reserved" seats, with a tradition of Catholic and Jewish representation. In 2022, Ketanji Brown Jackson became the first African American woman Justice, joining a Court that has become increasingly diverse while maintaining its elite educational homogeneity.

Fig. 9 Current members of SCOTUS (appointed by Conservative presidents are underlined)

Name	Appointed By (Year)	Birth Year	Ideological Tendency	Law School / Clerkship / Ethnicity
John G. Roberts, Jr. (Chief Justice)	W. Bush (2005)	1955	Conservative	Harvard Law, Clerked for William Rehnquist
Clarence Thomas	H.W. Bush (1991)	1948	Conservative	Yale Law, Black, divorced, Anita Hill
Samuel A. Alito, Jr.	W. Bush (2006)	1950	Conservative	Yale Law, Italian, Catholic

Sonia Sotomayor	Obama (2009)	1954	Liberal	Yale Law, Hispanic
Elena Kagan	Obama (2010)	1960	Liberal	Harvard Law, Jewish, clerked for Thurgood Marshall
Neil M. Gorsuch	Trump (2017)	1967	Conservative	Harvard Law, Oxford, clerked for Byron White/Anthony Kennedy
Brett M. Kavanaugh	Trump (2018)	1965	Conservative	Yale Law, Irish Catholic, clerked for Anthony Kennedy
Amy Coney Barrett	Trump (2020)	1972	Conservative	Notre Dame, Catholic, clerked for Antonin Scalia
Ketanji Brown Jackson	Biden (2022)	1970	Liberal	Harvard Law, Black, clerked for Stephen Breyer

4. Highly Political Nature of the Confirmation Hearing

The Supreme Court nomination process has transformed into an intensely partisan battleground, shaped by several watershed moments. The 1987 rejection of Robert Bork marked the first major shift, as his extensive written record and conservative ideology proved fatal to his confirmation. This experience led to the subsequent nomination of David Souter in 1990, deliberately chosen for his minimal paper trail. However, Souter's eventual evolution into a reliable liberal vote served as a cautionary tale for presidents seeking ideological certainty in their nominees.

These experiences fundamentally altered the nomination strategy, with presidents now "grooming" potential nominees early in their careers while carefully managing their public positions. The process has become increasingly partisan, as evidenced by Senate Republicans' 2016 blockade of Merrick Garland's nomination and the rushed confirmation of Amy Coney Barrett in 2020.

The death of Ruth Bader Ginsburg during Trump's presidency proved particularly consequential, shifting the Court's ideological balance to a 6-3 conservative majority. This event has intensified calls for aging justices to consider strategic retirement during ideologically aligned presidencies, potentially compromising the tradition of life tenure. Critics argue that such political calculations about retirement timing threaten the Court's independence and institutional integrity, while others contend they reflect a necessary adaptation to modern political realities.

These developments highlight how Supreme Court nominations have evolved from evaluations of judicial qualification to high-stakes political battles that can reshape American jurisprudence for generations.

5. Decision making process at the Supreme Court

1) Briefing

Cases begin with parties filing briefs and reply briefs, limited to 50 pages, outlining arguments and relevant precedents. Interest groups may file amicus curiae briefs, while Court clerks prepare additional background materials for the Justices.

2) Oral Argument

Each side receives 30 minutes to present their case, though proceedings are largely driven by Justices' questions. Following oral arguments, Justices make preliminary decisions, though these may evolve during later deliberations.

3) Conference

In closed-door sessions, the Chief Justice presents each case's facts, history, and disposition. Justices speak in order of seniority and vote on the merits. Despite its formal structure, these sessions rarely involve negotiation.

4) Opinion Assignment

The Chief Justice, if in the majority, or the senior Justice in the majority assigns opinion writing. Assignments consider workload, ideological alignment, and specific expertise. Justices may also volunteer for assignments.

5) Opinion Writing

Law clerks typically draft initial opinions under Justice supervision. Drafts circulate for endorsement or suggested revisions. Coalition dynamics may shift as Justices negotiate specific language and holdings.

6) Announcement

The Court announces decisions from the bench, presenting majority opinions alongside any plurality, concurring, or dissenting opinions. These published opinions become binding precedent for lower courts.

6. Principles of Judicial Restraint in American Courts

American courts have developed a set of self-imposed limitations that guide when and how they exercise judicial power. These principles of judicial restraint help maintain the separation of powers and ensure that courts focus on genuine legal disputes rather than abstract policy questions. These principles of judicial restraint, developed over time, help define the proper role of courts in American democracy while preserving their essential function as guardians of constitutional rights.

1) The Case or Controversy Requirement

Courts will only hear cases involving actual disputes between parties with concrete interests at stake. This means three key requirements must be met: First, there must be a real controversy, not a hypothetical question. Second, the parties must have proper standing, meaning they have suffered actual harm that the court can remedy. Third, the issue must not be moot – the court's decision must be able to affect the current situation.

For example, courts generally won't give advisory opinions about potential future laws or hypothetical situations. However, state courts may sometimes issue declaratory judgments to clarify legal rights before a dispute escalates to litigation.

2) Specificity in Constitutional Challenges

When challenging a law's constitutionality, petitioners must identify specific constitutional provisions that the law allegedly violates. General complaints about a law's fairness or wisdom are insufficient. The Supreme Court demonstrated this principle when upholding Ohio's school scholarship program that included religious schools. While challengers claimed this violated the Establishment Clause, the Court found the connection too indirect since funds went to parents rather than religious institutions directly.

3) Limitations on Appellate Review

Appellate courts focus on questions of law rather than re-examining factual determinations made by trial courts. This division of labor helps maintain efficient judicial administration while ensuring legal principles are applied consistently. While the Supreme Court technically isn't bound by its own precedents, it generally follows them unless there are compelling reasons for change.

4) The Political Question Doctrine

Courts refrain from deciding issues that properly belong to the political branches of government. This includes questions about foreign policy, partisan political disputes, and matters the Constitution assigns to Congress or the Executive. A clear example occurred in 2003 when Texas Democrats fled the state to prevent a vote on redistricting. Courts declined to intervene, viewing it as a political rather than legal dispute.

5) Judicial Modesty in Constitutional Review

When reviewing legislation, courts follow several principles of restraint. They place the burden of proof on those challenging the law's constitutionality. If possible, they decide cases on narrow statutory grounds rather than broad constitutional ones. When finding laws unconstitutional, they try to invalidate only the specific problematic provisions rather than striking down entire statutes.

Perhaps most importantly, courts avoid judging the wisdom of legislation, focusing instead on its constitutionality. As Justice Potter Stewart noted in his Griswold v. Connecticut dissent, a law may be "uncommonly silly" yet still constitutional. This restraint helps maintain the distinction between legal and political decision-making while respecting the legislature's primary role in making policy choices.

CHAPTER XII. SCOTUS AND SOCIAL CHANGE – WARREN COURT ERA

1. Warren Court and Civil Rights Movement

The Warren Court (1953-1969) fundamentally transformed American society through landmark decisions that expanded civil rights and individual liberties. Under Chief Justice Earl Warren's leadership, despite being appointed by Republican Eisenhower, the Court issued groundbreaking rulings in cases like Brown v. Board of Education, Miranda v. Arizona, and Gideon v. Wainwright, establishing the Court as an engine of progressive social change.

The Court nonetheless is considered controversial for its perceived judicial activism and broad interpretation of constitutional rights, leading critics to accuse it of overstepping judicial boundaries and legislating from the bench. President Eisenhower later reportedly called his appointment of Warren "the biggest damn fool mistake" he ever made.

The era stands as a testament to how the Supreme Court can serve as a catalyst for social transformation, while also highlighting enduring tensions between judicial activism and restraint in American constitutional democracy.

The Warren Court (1953-69)	• Earl Warren was appointed by Dwight Eisenhower (Republican) – But, showed decisively liberal tendencies • Was the governor of California (after serving as the AG) – Supported Eisenhower and withdrew his candidacy in support of him • Many landmark cases came under his reign, including Brown, Mapp, Baker, etc.
The Burger Court (1969-86)	• Warren Burger appointed by Richard Nixon (R) - Conservative • Warren Court decisions were sometimes scaled back • More conservative than Warren Court but no counter-revolution – In the 80s, centrist justice block dominated the decisions

The Rehnquist Court (1986-2005)	• William Rehnquist appointed by Ronald Reagan (R) – Conservative
	• Slow move towards right
	  – "Court no longer a social engine"
	  – More role to the states

The Roberts Court (2005-)	• John Roberts appointed by George W. Bush (R) – Conservative • Clerked for Rehnquist and similar to Rehnquist in ideological molding

Fig. 10 SCOTUS eras by Chief Justice

2. Earl Warren and his Appointment to SCOTUS

Earl Warren, the 14th Chief Justice of the U. S. Supreme Court from 1953-1969, was Governor of California and was instrumental in securing Republican nomination for Dwight Eisenhower's in 1952. He was promised an appointment to the next available Supreme Court vacancy by Eisenhower. After Ike won the presidential election the next opening occurred after Fred Vinson's unexpected death. President Eisenhower wanted to go back on his word because he didn't expect the next opening to be the Chief Justice. But "Warren gave the president an ultimatum: appoint him to the first vacancy, as promised, or he would resign as governor and stomp the nation, denouncing the president as a liar. The following month, Ike nominated Warren to the nation's highest judicial office." This decision led to an era of judicial revolution under the leadership of Warren.

This appointment, born from political maneuvering rather than traditional judicial credentials, would prove transformative. Warren, despite his lack of prior judicial experience, went on to lead the Court through its most progressive era, fundamentally reshaping American constitutional law and civil rights.

How a Republican governor became a civil rights crusader requires analysis into his background. Despite being identified as a "conservative" Republican, Warren hailed from California's Progressive Republican tradition, which blended efficiency in government with social-minded reform. As a governor, he supported the forced removal and internment of Japanese Americans during World War II. He is said to have deeply regretted over the decision. Once he became Chief Justice, Warren's sense of duty to constitutional equality and fairness influenced him to lead pivotal decisions expanding civil rights.

3. Milestone Cases of Warren Court - Expanding Civil Rights and Civil Liberties

These landmark decisions reflect the Warren Court's broader commitment to expanding civil rights and liberties while ensuring greater procedural fairness in the criminal justice system. Though some decisions proved controversial at the time, many have become foundational principles of American constitutional law that continue to shape legal debates today.

1) Brown v. Board of Education, 347 U.S. 483 (1954) - Civil Rights/Equal Protection (also See Chapter XIII Travails of Racial Equality)

Facts: Linda Brown was a young African American student who had to walk five miles to attend a segregated black school, despite living much closer to a white school. The NAACP, led by Thurgood Marshall, challenged school segregation in Topeka, Kansas, arguing that "separate but equal" facilities violated the Equal Protection Clause of the 14th Amendment.

Ruling: In a unanimous decision written by Chief Justice Warren, the Court held that separate educational facilities were "inherently unequal." The Court found that segregation generated feelings of inferiority in minority children that could "affect their hearts and minds in a way unlikely ever to be undone." The decision overturned Plessy v. Ferguson's "separate but equal" doctrine and became the legal foundation of the civil rights movement. While implementation proved challenging, as evidenced by the subsequent "all deliberate speed" standard in Brown II (1955), the ruling fundamentally changed American society and constitutional law.

2) Mapp v. Ohio, 367 U.S. 643 (1961) - Criminal Procedure/Fourth Amendment

Facts: Police officers, believing a bombing suspect was hiding in Dollree Mapp's home, forced their way in without a valid search warrant. Although they didn't find the suspect, they discovered allegedly obscene materials and arrested Mapp. She was convicted based on this evidence despite the illegal search.

Ruling: The Court held that evidence obtained through unconstitutional searches and seizures is inadmissible in state courts, extending the federal exclusionary rule to state proceedings through the Fourth and Fourteenth Amendments. The decision revolutionized American criminal procedure by providing a strong incentive for police to obtain proper warrants. It established the principle that the same constitutional standards for searches apply to both federal and state law enforcement.

3) Miranda v. Arizona, 384 U.S. 436 (1966) - Criminal Procedure/Fifth Amendment

Facts: Ernesto Miranda was arrested for kidnapping and rape. After two hours of police interrogation, he signed a confession. He was not informed of his right to remain silent, his right to an attorney, or that his statements could be used against him.

Ruling: The Court established that police must inform suspects of their constitutional rights before custodial interrogation. These rights include the right to remain silent, that statements can be used against them, the right to an attorney, and the right to have one appointed if they cannot afford one. The decision fundamentally changed law enforcement practices and created the now-familiar "Miranda warnings." Though controversial at the time, these warnings have become a deeply embedded part of American legal culture and police procedure.

4) Katz v. United States, 389 U.S. 347 (1967) - Privacy Rights/Fourth Amendment

Facts: FBI agents attached an electronic listening device to the outside of a public phone booth that Charles Katz regularly used to transmit gambling information. The FBI recorded his conversations without obtaining a warrant, arguing that no physical intrusion occurred.

Ruling: The Court overturned Olmstead v. United States and held that the Fourth Amendment protects people, not places. Justice Harlan's influential concurrence established the "reasonable expectation of privacy" test that continues to guide Fourth Amendment analysis. The decision modernized Fourth Amendment protections for the electronic age and established that constitutional privacy rights exist even in publicly accessible spaces. The ruling's principles continue to shape debates about privacy rights in the face of evolving technology.

5) Engel v. Vitale, 370 U.S. 421 (1962) - First Amendment/Establishment Clause

Facts: The New York State Board of Regents composed a nondenominational prayer and recommended that public schools begin each day with its recitation. The prayer read: "Almighty God, we acknowledge our dependence upon Thee, and we beg Thy blessings upon us, our parents, our teachers, and our Country." Though the prayer was technically voluntary, parents of ten students challenged the practice.

Ruling: In a 6-1 decision, the Court held that state-sponsored prayer in public schools violated the Establishment Clause of the First Amendment, even if the prayer was denominationally neutral and students could choose not to participate. The decision established a strong precedent against state-sponsored religious activities in public schools and reinforced the separation of church and state. It sparked significant public controversy and remains influential in debates about religion in public education.

6) Abington School District v. Schempp, 374 U.S. 203 (1963) - First Amendment/Establishment Clause

Facts: A Pennsylvania law required that schools begin each day with Bible readings. The Schempp family, who were Unitarians, challenged the law as a violation of the First Amendment's Establishment Clause. The school argued that the readings were nonreligious moral and literary exercises.

Ruling: The Court held that school-sponsored Bible reading and recitation of the Lord's Prayer in public schools violated the Establishment Clause. The Court established the "secular purpose" test: that laws must have a secular legislative purpose and a primary effect that neither advances nor inhibits religion. Together with Engel, this decision helped define the modern understanding of church-state separation in public education and established key principles for analyzing

Establishment Clause cases.

7) Tinker v. Des Moines Independent Community School District, 393 U.S. 503 (1969) - First Amendment/Student Rights

Facts: In December 1965, several students, including John and Mary Beth Tinker, planned to wear black armbands to school to protest the Vietnam War. School officials learned of the plan and adopted a policy prohibiting armbands. When the students wore them anyway, they were suspended.

Ruling: The Court held that students do not "shed their constitutional rights to freedom of speech or expression at the schoolhouse gate." Schools cannot suppress student expression unless they can reasonably forecast that it will materially and substantially disrupt school operations. The decision established strong First Amendment protections for student speech and expression. The "Tinker test" continues to be the standard for evaluating restrictions on student speech, though subsequent decisions have carved out exceptions.

8) Gideon v. Wainwright and Right to Counsel/Sixth Amendment

1) Gideon v. Wainwright, 372 U.S. 335 (1963)

Facts: Clarence Earl Gideon was charged with breaking and entering in Florida state court. When he requested a court-appointed attorney, the judge denied his request because Florida only provided attorneys for defendants charged with capital offenses. Gideon defended himself, was convicted, and sent to prison.

Ruling: The Court unanimously held that the Sixth Amendment's guarantee of counsel is a fundamental right essential to a fair trial and applies to the states through the Fourteenth Amendment. States must provide attorneys for criminal defendants who cannot afford them. The decision dramatically expanded access to justice and led to the creation of public defender systems nationwide. It represents one of the Warren Court's most important efforts to ensure fair treatment for all defendants regardless of economic status.

2) Evolution of the Right to Counsel in American Criminal Justice

Gideon v. Wainwright overturned Betts v. Brady in a series of landmark Supreme Court decisions in the mid-20th century that established the right to legal representation in criminal case. This evolution reflects the Court's growing recognition that meaningful access to counsel is essential for a fair trial.

(1) Betts v. Brady (1942): The Limited Right

The Supreme Court initially took a restrictive view of the right to counsel in Betts v. Brady. When Smith Betts was denied a court-appointed attorney for his robbery trial in Maryland, the Court upheld the conviction, ruling that states only needed to provide counsel in special circumstances. This case-by-case approach meant that many defendants faced criminal charges without legal representation simply because they couldn't afford it. The Court reasoned that the Sixth Amendment's right to counsel did not automatically apply to state courts through the Fourteenth Amendment.

(2) Escobedo v. Illinois (1964): Extending Protection to Police Interrogation

After Gideon v. Wainwright, the Court further expanded defendants' rights in Escobedo v. Illinois, 378 U.S. 478 (1964) by focusing on the critical pre-trial period. Danny Escobedo confessed to murder after police denied his repeated requests to speak with his lawyer during interrogation. The Court overturned his conviction, establishing what became known as the "Escobedo Rule": suspects have a right to counsel once an investigation focuses on them as particular suspects.

This decision recognized that the right to counsel must extend beyond the courtroom to police interrogations, where critical evidence is often obtained. The Court understood that without legal advice during questioning, defendants might unknowingly compromise their defense before trial even begins.

These cases transformed American criminal justice by establishing that the right to counsel is not a luxury reserved for the wealthy but a fundamental right necessary for fair proceedings. The decisions recognized that legal representation is essential at both trial and critical pre-trial stages. While implementation challenges remain, particularly regarding the quality of appointed counsel, these rulings established crucial constitutional protections that continue to shape criminal procedure today.

""

CHAPTER XIII. TRAVAILS OF RACIAL EQUALITY

The journey toward racial equality in American law, marked by periods of progress and regression, demonstrates both the potential and limitations of using legal institutions to achieve social change. Through examining key Supreme Court decisions, we can trace how American jurisprudence has grappled with questions of race, citizenship, and equality under law.

1. Origins of Legal Inequality

Slavery in America began as an economic institution but developed into a complex legal and social system. While various forms of servitude existed throughout human history, American chattel slavery was distinct in its comprehensive denial of human rights and its racial basis. Unlike bonded labor or forced labor systems where some legal rights remained intact, chattel slavery treated humans as literal property - a status enforced and protected by law.

When European colonizers arrived in the Americas, the decimation of indigenous populations through disease and conflict created an acute labor shortage. This economic pressure, combined with existing African slave trade networks, led to the systematic importation of enslaved Africans. The legal framework that developed around slavery would have long-lasting implications for American jurisprudence.

2. Supreme Court Decisions

1) The Dred Scott Decision, 60 U.S. (19 How.) 393 (1857)

(1) Facts and procedural history

Dred Scott (pictured) was born into slavery in Virginia around 1800. In 1832, he was purchased by U.S. Army Major John Emerson, who was stationed near St. Louis. Throughout Emerson's military service, he took Scott to various postings, including territories where slavery was prohibited by state law (Illinois) and federal law (Wisconsin Territory). During this period, Scott was permitted to marry, a right not typically granted to enslaved persons under common law. When Emerson retired from the army in 1842, he had married Eliza Sanford. Upon Emerson's death in 1843, his estate, including Scott, passed to his widow. Scott attempted to purchase freedom for himself and his family, but Eliza Sanford refused.

After unsuccessful challenges through Missouri state court and New York federal court, Scott appealed to the Supreme Court. The legal issues where whether:
- Scott, as a person of African descent, has standing to sue in federal court?
- His residence in a free territory confer freedom upon an enslaved person?
- Congress has the authority to prohibit slavery in federal territories?

(2) Supreme Court ruling

In rejecting Scott's argument that he was a citizen entitled to sue in federal court, as his residency was in the free territories, Chief Justice Taney (pictured) wrote the majority opinion that went far beyond the specific facts of the case to make sweeping pronouncements about the status of African Americans under the Constitution.

The Court held that African Americans, whether enslaved or free, could not be American citizens and therefore had no standing to sue in federal court. Further, the Court ruled that Congress lacked authority to prohibit slavery in federal territories, effectively invalidating the Missouri Compromise.

Taney's opinion explicitly endorsed white supremacy, declaring that African Americans were "beings of an inferior order" unsuited for association with whites.

(3) Impact of the decision

This decision not only denied basic rights to African Americans but also eliminated any possibility of a legislative compromise over slavery's expansion. By constitutionalizing slavery and white supremacy, it has been said that the Court helped precipitate the Civil War.

2) Plessy v. Ferguson, 163 U.S. 537 (1896)

(1) Facts and procedural history

Homer Plessy, who was seven-eighths white and one-eighth black, purchased a first-class ticket on the East Louisiana Railroad and sat in a car designated for white passengers. Under Louisiana's Separate Car Act of 1890, Plessy was legally classified as Black despite his predominantly white ancestry, and therefore required to sit in the "colored" car. In what was a planned act of civil disobedience to test the law's constitutionality, Plessy refused to move to the segregated car. He was subsequently arrested and jailed for violating the state's segregation statute.

At trial, Judge John Howard Ferguson ruled in favor of the state, holding that Louisiana had the constitutional authority to regulate railroad companies operating within state boundaries. Plessy sought a writ of prohibition from the Louisiana Supreme Court, which upheld Ferguson's ruling. The case was then appealed to the U.S. Supreme Court.

Plessy contended that forced segregation violated his rights under both the Thirteenth and Fourteenth Amendments, imposed a badge of inferiority on African

Americans, and created an unconstitutional distinction based on race.

(2) Supreme Court ruling

The Court rejected Plessy's argument, siding with the state that argued that the law was a reasonable exercise of state police power, that separate facilities could be equal in quality, thus establishing the "separate but equal" doctrine that would justify racial segregation for the next half-century, and that the social equality was not a constitutional right.

Justice Brown's majority opinion held that segregation did not imply racial inferiority and that any such inference came solely from African Americans' interpretation of the law. Only Justice Harlan dissented, famously declaring that the "Constitution is color-blind."

(3) Impact of the decision

The Plessy decision gave constitutional sanction to the emerging system of Jim Crow laws across the South. While theoretically requiring equality in separate facilities, in practice the doctrine was used to maintain systematic inequality while providing a veneer of constitutional legitimacy.

3) Brown v. Board of Education, 347 U.S. 483 (1954)

(1) Facts and procedural history

In 1951, thirteen parents filed a class action lawsuit against the Board of Education of Topeka, Kansas, on behalf of their twenty children, including Oliver Brown. The suit called for the school district to reverse its policy of racial segregation. Separate elementary schools were operated by the Topeka Board of Education under an 1879 Kansas law, which permitted (but did not require) districts to maintain separate elementary school facilities for black and white students in twelve communities with populations over 15,000.

The plaintiffs filed a class-action lawsuit against the Topeka Board of Education, arguing that segregation in public schools was unconstitutional. After

losing in the district court, they appealed to the Supreme Court, represented by NAACP chief counsel Thurgood Marshall. Legal issues presented were:
- Does state-mandated racial segregation in public schools violate the Equal Protection Clause of the Fourteenth Amendment, even when physical facilities and other tangible factors are equal?
- Is the "separate but equal" doctrine established in Plessy v. Ferguson constitutionally valid in the context of public education?

(2) Supreme Court ruling

In a unanimous decision, the Court held that even if segregated black and white schools were of equal quality in facilities and teachers, segregation by itself was harmful to black students and unconstitutional. They found that a significant psychological and social disadvantage was given to black children from the nature of segregation itself. This aspect was vital because the question was not whether the schools were "equal", which under Plessy, but whether the doctrine of separate was constitutional.

(3) Impact of the decision

The decision effectively overturned Plessy v. Ferguson in the context of public education and marked the beginning of the end for legal segregation in the United States. The case became the legal foundation for the civil rights movement and led to subsequent civil rights legislation. The Brown decision's significance extends beyond its specific holding. By rejecting the formalistic equality of Plessy in favor of examining actual social effects, the Court opened new possibilities for using constitutional law to address racial discrimination. The ruling provided crucial legal foundation for the civil rights movement and subsequent civil rights legislation.

However, the implementation challenges that followed, as evidenced by Brown II's "all deliberate speed" standard, demonstrated the complex relationship between legal doctrine and social change. The NCAA attorney that handled this case, Thurgood Marshall (pictured in the middle) became the first black Supreme Court Justice in 1967, nominated by President Lyndon B. Johnson.

CHAPTER XIV. 14th AMENDMENT PROTECTION OF CIVIL RIGHTS

The Fourteenth Amendment, ratified in 1868 during Reconstruction, became the most powerful legal tool for advancing civil rights in American history. Its key provisions - the Equal Protection Clause and the Due Process Clause - required states to provide equal protection under law and prohibited them from depriving any person of life, liberty, or property without due process. Initially enacted to protect the rights of formerly enslaved people after the Civil War, the Amendment's scope expanded dramatically through Supreme Court interpretation. The Court used it to incorporate most Bill of Rights protections against state governments and to strike down various forms of discrimination, most notably racial segregation in Brown v. Board of Education (1954). The Amendment remains central to contemporary civil rights litigation, protecting everything from voting rights to marriage equality. Its two key provisions - the Due Process Clause and the Equal Protection Clause - have become fundamental tools for protecting civil rights against state infringement. The 14th Amendment states in the relevant part (Section 1):

"Nor shall any state deprive any person of life, liberty, or property, without due process of law, nor deny any person within its jurisdiction the equal protection of the laws."

1. Due Process of Law

The Due Process Clause declares that no state shall "deprive any person of life, liberty, or property, without due process of law." Courts have interpreted this clause to provide two distinct types of protection: procedural and substantive due process.

1) Procedural Due Process

Procedural due process requires states to provide fair procedures before depriving individuals of protected interests. At its core, this means notice and an opportunity to be heard. The Supreme Court has established specific requirements through cases like Goldberg v. Kelly (1970), which required hearings before terminating welfare benefits, and Mathews v. Eldridge (1976), which created a three-part test for determining what procedures are required in different contexts. These protections ensure that government actions affecting individual rights follow fair and established processes.

2) Substantive Due Process

Beyond procedural protections, courts have interpreted the Due Process Clause to protect certain fundamental rights from government interference regardless of what procedures are followed. This doctrine of substantive due process began with economic rights in cases like Lochner v. New York (1905) but evolved to protect personal autonomy and privacy. Landmark cases include Griswold v. Connecticut (1965) protecting contraceptive use, Roe v. Wade (1973) establishing abortion rights, and Obergefell v. Hodges (2015) recognizing same-sex marriage. While controversial, substantive due process remains a crucial tool for protecting unenumerated rights.

2. Equal Protection

The Equal Protection Clause requires states to treat similarly situated people alike. Courts have developed a three-tiered system of scrutiny to evaluate different types of government classifications:

1) Strict scrutiny

Strict scrutiny applies to classifications based on race, national origin, and fundamental rights. Government actions must be narrowly tailored to serve a compelling state interest. Most laws fail this demanding test, as demonstrated in cases like Loving v. Virginia (1967) striking down bans on interracial marriage.

2) Intermediate scrutiny

Intermediate scrutiny applies to gender-based classifications, requiring them to be substantially related to an important government interest. This standard has been used to invalidate many gender discriminatory laws while allowing some sex-based distinctions, as seen in Craig v. Boren (1976).

3) Rational basis review

Rational basis review applies to most other classifications, requiring only that they be rationally related to a legitimate government purpose. While this standard is usually deferential, it has been used to strike down laws based on pure animus, as in Romer v. Evans (1996).

3. Incorporation Doctrine

The Fourteenth Amendment has also been the vehicle for applying most Bill of Rights protections to the states through "selective incorporation." This process began with First Amendment freedoms in Gitlow v. New York (1925) and continued through cases like Mapp v. Ohio (1961) incorporating Fourth Amendment protections and Gideon v. Wainwright (1963) requiring states to provide counsel to criminal defendants. This doctrine has fundamentally reshaped state criminal procedure and civil liberties.

AM	Rights	Incorporated	Not incorporated
1st AM	Establishment of religion	Everson v. Board of Ed. (1947)	
	Free exercise of religion	Cantwell v. Connecticut (1940)	
	Freedom of speech	Gitlow v. New York (1925)	
	Freedom of the press	Near v. Minnesota (1931)	
	Freedom of assembly	DeJonge v. Oregon (1937)	
2nd AM	Right to keep and bear arms	McDonald v. City of Chicago (2010)	
3rd AM	Freedom from quartering of soldiers	Within the Second Circuit	the states elsewhere
4th AM	Unreasonable search and seizure	Mapp v. Ohio (1961)	
	Warrant requirements	Aguilar v. Texas (1964)	
5th AM	Indictment by a grand jury		Hurtado v. California (1884)
	Double jeopardy	Benton v. Maryland (1969)	
	Against self-incrimination	Griffin v. California (1965)	
	Just compensation for taking of private property	Chicago, Burlington & Quincy RR Co. v. City of Chicago (1897)	

4. Modern Applications and Debates

Today, the Fourteenth Amendment continues to be at the center of civil rights controversies. Recent cases have addressed issues like affirmative action in Fisher v. University of Texas (2016), voting rights in Shelby County v. Holder (2013), and

LGBTQ+ rights in Bostock v. Clayton County (2020). Ongoing debates focus on how to balance individual rights with state interests in areas like public health measures, election administration, and emerging technologies.

The Amendment's broad language and adaptable principles ensure it will remain crucial for protecting civil rights as society evolves. While interpretations may shift, its fundamental guarantee of due process and equal protection continues to serve as a cornerstone of American constitutional democracy.

- **EPILOGUE**

The Anglo-American legal system represents a fascinating intersection of historical evolution, philosophical principles, and practical adaptations to societal needs. From its origins in medieval English boroughs through its development into a sophisticated mechanism for resolving modern disputes, common law has demonstrated remarkable resilience and adaptability.

Unlike civil law systems that emerged from systematic academic study and codification of Roman law, common law evolved organically through case-by-case adjudication. This bottom-up development created a distinctly practical approach to justice, one that prioritizes real-world problem-solving over theoretical elegance. The system's emphasis on precedent (stare decisis) provides stability while allowing for incremental evolution as society changes.

The transplantation of English common law to American soil produced further innovations. The American experiment added written constitutionalism and judicial review to the common law tradition, creating a hybrid system that combines the flexibility of case law with the stability of constitutional principles. This fusion proved particularly powerful in addressing social change, as demonstrated during the Warren Court era when constitutional interpretation became a powerful tool for advancing civil rights.

A defining characteristic of the Anglo-American system is its ability to balance competing demands. The tension between stability and change, between individual rights and collective welfare, and between federal and state authority has produced sophisticated legal doctrines that can accommodate diverse societal needs. The development of due process and equal protection jurisprudence under the Fourteenth Amendment illustrates how the system can generate nuanced solutions to complex social problems.

Looking ahead, the Anglo-American legal system faces several critical challenges. First, rapid technological advancement raises novel questions about privacy, property rights, and regulatory frameworks that test traditional common law principles. The system must adapt to address issues like artificial intelligence, cryptocurrency, and digital privacy while maintaining its fundamental commitment to justice and fairness.

Second, increasing globalization challenges the territorial nature of traditional legal authority. As transactions and disputes increasingly cross national boundaries, the common law system must find ways to coordinate with other legal traditions while preserving its essential characteristics.

Finally, growing social inequality and political polarization test the system's ability to maintain legitimacy and deliver justice fairly. The legal system must evolve to ensure access to justice remains meaningful for all members of society, not just those with resources to navigate its complexities.

Despite these challenges, the historical record suggests the Anglo-American legal system will continue to adapt and evolve. Its fundamental strengths - practical problem-solving, incremental development through precedent, and the ability to balance competing interests - provide tools for addressing future challenges. The system's capacity for self-correction and reform, though sometimes slow, has proven remarkably durable over centuries of social change.

The future likely holds continued evolution rather than revolution, with courts and legislatures working to adapt existing principles to new circumstances while preserving the core values that have made the system effective. The key will be maintaining the delicate balance between stability and change that has characterized the system's development from its medieval origins to its current sophistication.

""

Editor:
Prof.   Ryan S. Song
South Korea

© 2024. EduContentsHuepia Books.

All rights reserved including those of translation into other languages. No part of this book may be reprinted or reproduced in any form – by photoprinting, microfilm, or any other means – nor transmitted or translated into machine language without written permission from the author.

Registered names, trademarks, etc. used in this book, even when not specifically marked as such, are not to be considered unprotected by law.

First edition on **December 30th, 2024**
Identifiers: ISBN **978-89-6356-488-3**